Lexical Categories in Spanish

The Determiner

Linda M. McManness

University Press of America, Inc.
Lanham • New York • London

Copyright © 1996 by
University Press of America,® Inc.
4720 Boston Way
Lanham, Maryland 20706

3 Henrietta Street
London, WC2E 8LU England

All rights reserved
Printed in the United States of America
British Cataloging in Publication Information Available

Library of Congress Cataloging-in-Publication Data

McManness, Linda M.
Lexical categories in Spanish : the determiner / Linda M. McManness.
p.   cm.
Includes bibliographical references and indexes.
1. Spanish language--Determiners. 2. Government--binding theory
(Linguistics). I. Title.
PC4398.D47M3   1995   465 --dc20   95-38845 CIP

ISBN 0-7618-0137-5 (cloth : alk: ppr.)

♾ The paper used in this publication meets the minimum
requirements of American National Standard for information
Sciences—Permanence of Paper for Printed Library Materials,
ANSI Z39.48—1984

To Grady Wray, Thank you for being my friend

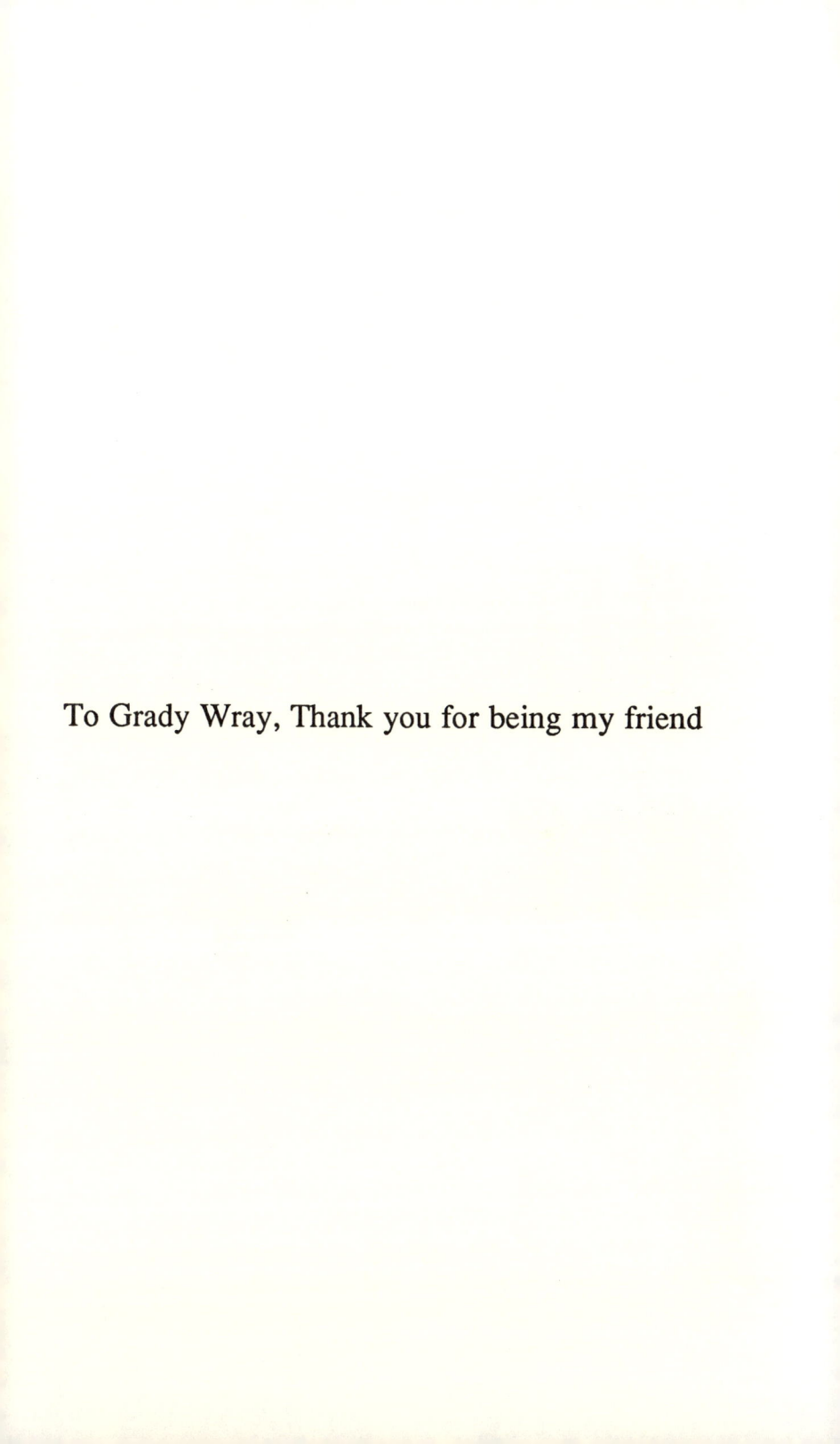

Contents

PREFACE	ix
ACKNOWLEDGEMENTS	xi
CHAPTER 1: THEORETICAL BACKGROUND	1
1.0. Introduction	1
1.1. Government-Binding Theory	2
1.1.2. X'Theory	4
1.1.3. Theta Theory	6
1.1.4. Case Theory	8
1.1.5. Government	9
1.1.6. Binding Theory	10
1.1.7. Control Theory	11
1.1.8. Conclusions	11
1.2. Overview	12
Notes to Chapter 1	12
CHAPTER 2: GENERAL THEORETICAL ASSUMPTIONS ABOUT DETERMINER PHRASES	13
2.0. Introduction	13
2.1. Abney's DP Hypothesis	15
2.1.1. Motivation for the DP Hypothesis	15
2.1.2. Similarities Between Noun Phrases and Sentences	16
2.1.3. Differences Between Noun Phrases and Sentences	18
2.1.4. The Structure of DP	20
2.1.5. Functional versus Thematic Elements	22
2.1.6. PRO in NP (DP)	24
2.2. Analysis of Fukui and Speas (1986)	26
2.2.1. Properties of Functional Categories	28
2.2.2. Movement	29
2.3. Critique of Abney and Fukui and Speas	31

2.3.1. Critique of Abney	31
2.3.2. Discussion of Abney with regard to Spanish	31
2.3.3. Discussion of Functional Categories	33
2.3.4. Differences between Spanish and English DPs	34
2.3.5. Critique of Fukui and Speas	34
2.3.6. The Determiner as a Functional Category	35
2.4. Proposal of Determiner as a Lexical Category in Spanish	36
2.4.1. Motivation for the Proposal	36
2.4.2. Iteration of Determiners in Spanish	36
2.4.3. Structure of Determiner Phrases	37
2.5. Conclusions	38
Notes to Chapter 2	38
CHAPTER 3: DEMONSTRATIVES AND DEFINITE ARTICLES	41
3.0. Introduction	41
3.1. The Definite Article	41
3.1.1. Omission of the Definite Article	42
3.1.2. Gender and Number of the Definite Article	42
3.1.3. Uses of the Definite Article	43
3.1.4. Definite Article without a Noun	43
3.2. Torrego's Analysis of Empty Noun Phrases	44
3.2.1. Restrictions on *el* Nominals	44
3.2.2. The *el* Nominal versus the *este* Nominal	45
3.2.3. Categorizing the Empty Element in a Nominal	46
3.2.4. 'Strong' versus 'Weak' Determiners	46
3.2.5. PPs with *el* Nominals	47
3.2.6. Empty Nominal Structure	48
3.2.7. The Referent of pro in *el* Nominals	49
3.3. Critique of Torrego's Analysis	50
3.4. Bosque's Analysis of Empty Nominals	51
3.5. Contreras' Analysis of Empty Nominals	53
3.5.1. Problems with the Specifier-as-Proper-Governor Analysis	53
3.5.2. Empirical Data Contra Bosque	54
3.5.3. Theoretical Considerations	55

3.5.4. Binding Theory Considerations	55
3.5.5. The Determiner as a Functional Head	56
3.5.6. Theoretical Considerations	56
3.5.7. Advantages to the Determiner-as-Functional-Head	57
3.5.8. A Parallel Situation: The Quantifier as Head of Phrase	57
3.6. Discussion of Contreras (1989)	59
3.7. Definite Article in Subject Position	60
3.7.1. Contreras' (1986) Analysis of Bare NPs	60
3.7.2. Spanish as a VOS Language	60
3.7.3. Accounting for SVO Word Order	61
3.7.4. Accounting for Plural NPs without Determiners	61
3.7.5. Plural Bare Nouns in Topic Position	62
3.7.6. Empty QPs with Mass Nouns	62
3.7.7. Evidence for a Parallelism Condition	63
3.7.8. Proper Government of Spanish Bare NPs	64
3.8. Discussion of Contreras (1986)	65
3.9. Conclusions	66
Notes to Chapter 3	66
CHAPTER 4: POSSESSIVES AND GENITIVES	69
4.0. Introduction	69
4.1. The Genitive Analysis of Chomsky (1986b)	70
4.2. Abney's Analysis of the English Genitive	70
4.3. Analysis of Abney with respect to Spanish	72
4.4. Fukui's Treatment of Genitive Case in English	74
4.5. Discussion of Fukui and Speas' Proposal for Genitive Case: Spanish versus English	74
4.6. Mallén's Proposal for Possessive Phrases	77
4.6.1. The Structure of QP	78
4.6.2. Possessives and Ex-versus In-arguments	79
4.6.3. Genitive Case and θ role for Spanish NPs	80
4.6.4. Pronominal Possessives	81
4.6.5. The Character of QUAN	83
4.6.6. Advantages of Mallén's Proposal	84
4.6.7. R-nominals versus P-nominals	86
4.7. Discussion of Mallén	89

4.8. Contreras' Discussion of Possessives Heading Empty Nominals	92
4.9. Discussion of Contreras	94
4.10. The Possessive Determiner as Lexical Category	94
4.11. Conclusions	95
Notes to Chapter 4	96
CHAPTER 5: CONCLUSIONS	97
BIBLIOGRAPHY	99
INDEX OF NAMES	103
INDEX OF SUBJECTS	105

Preface

One of the greatest changes in generative theory has been the shift from the notion of language as a set of rules that vary from one language to another to the view of language as a more general set of universal principles that constrain the parameterization of a specific language. The parameters that individual languages possess are still subject to investigation and in this work, the differences between determiner phrases in English and Spanish will be examined.

The underlying framework for this study is Abney's (1987) hypothesis that the noun phrase is actually a determiner phrase (DP) with a structure similar to that of the sentence. The determiner, which heads its own phrase, is characterized by Abney as a functional category. Although the DP hypothesis is maintained in this work, there is evidence that the Spanish determiner is parameterized differently than that of English with respect to lexical versus functional categorization.

The central focus of this book is the hypothesis that the Spanish determiner is a lexical as opposed to a functional category. By refuting many of the claims made by Abney and Fukui and Speas (1986) regarding the determiner as a lexical category and by viewing the Spanish determiner as lexical, the proper government of empty categories and the assignment of genitive Case in Spanish DPs is accounted for in a more elegant and economical manner.

ACKNOWLEDGEMENTS

I would first like to thank all of my professors over the years but especially my dissertation advisor, Karen Zagona. Her knowledge of syntax and her advice in matters of writing were invaluable. Without her help and encouragement, this work would not have been possible.

A special thanks to Jurgen Klausenburger for introducing me to Romance linguistics and for all of his support during my graduate studies.

To Heles Contreras and Judith Strozer, I offer many thanks for their encouragement and linguistic insights throughout my years at the University of Washington.

Additionally, I would like to thank my native speaker informants Raúl Arteaga, Rafael Andrés Escribano-Díaz, and Lucía Llorente Gonzales for their time, help, and patience with my inquiries.

To all the friends and family members who believed in me but especially Grady Wray, Debbie Arteaga, Frieda Blackwell, Diane Dearmont, Mike Long, and Ann McGlashan, thanks for your unconditional love.

Chapter 1

Theoretical Background

1.0. INTRODUCTION

The quest of linguistic study continues to be a desire to explain what we mean when we say we know a language. The search is twofold: an investigation into how children acquire language so well in such a short period of time and the knowledge or competence that an adult speaker has which underlies the way in which he or she uses language. This linguistic competence is a cognitive structure that is presumably prewired in the brains of all humans and accounts for the unique ability of humans to acquire language. The Principles of language are the general rules that underlie all human languages. But the variations from language to language- the Parameters- are set by individual experience with that language by the child. The parametric variations from language to language will all still fall within the general principles of universal grammar (UG).

In this chapter we will examine the theoretical assumptions of the Government-Binding (GB) Theory as proposed in Chomsky (1981) that will be pertinent to the discussion of determiner phrases in this work. The modules of GB theory as well as definitions from Chomsky (1986b) that will prove useful in the chapters ahead will be reviewed. In addition to these topics, an overview of this study as a whole will be profiled.

1.1. GOVERNMENT-BINDING THEORY

In this section we will summarize the Government-Binding Theory (GB) as proposed by Chomsky (1981) and the various components that make up this theory. The subcomponents of universal grammar (UG) interact to produce the unique and grammatical utterances which are possible in a language. Below is a representation of the subcomponents of UG:

(1)
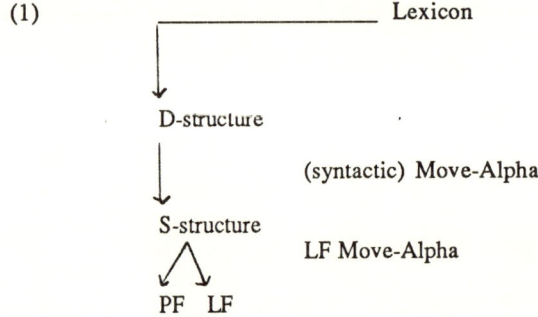

In order to better discuss the levels of representation and the rules that relate them, we can begin with the lexicon. The lexicon is the source of individual lexical items and contains phonological, syntactic and semantic information, the distinctive features and subcategorization of each item in a particular language. By subcategorization, the individual items in the lexicon are specified as to the type of thematic relations they can enter into with other items in the language. For example, a verb is subcategorized for the number and type of theta (θ) roles it can assign. Items in the lexicon then combine with each other at D-structure which is the level of representation where the thematic roles are actually assigned.

The transformational rule, Move-Alpha, is applied recursively and derives the S-structure from D-structure by moving elements into the order in which they occur in the spoken language. Alpha is simply an abbreviation for any category and the movement that results from the application of this rule will vary from language to language. For example, 'alpha' in English can represent a question word (a +wh element) which at D-structure is generated in the canonical object position following the verb but is in front of a clause at S-structure. The sentences in (2a) show the +wh word in its D-structure position where it receives its θ role from the verb. In (2b), Move-Alpha is applied to the +wh word, moving it to the front of the clause which gives the sentence an acceptable S-structure:

(2) a. She told me she saw [who].
  b. She told me [who] she saw.

The D-structure then is mapped onto S-structure through the application of Move-Alpha, however, S-structure interacts simultaneously with the other two components, PF and LF. S-structure gives the form or syntax to a particular phrase or sentence, PF gives the phonological form (sound), and LF, the logical form or meaning.

One final principle of GB theory must be obeyed in order for the syntactic levels which represent a particular sentence to relate to each other and this is known as the Projection Principle. This principle states that the sentence represented at each syntactic level (LF, D-structure, and S-structure) must have the same categorial elements. More formally, the definition of the Projection Principle from Chomsky (1981: 29):

(3) Representations at each syntactic level (i.e., LF, and D- and S-structure) are projected from the lexicon, in that they observe the subcategorization properties of lexical items.

For example, a verb like *to call* which subcategorizes for a direct object NP in the lexicon will have a direct object at D-structure, S-structure, and LF. Even if the direct object is not overtly expressed at S-structure, its position is still present. Therefore the S-structure in (2b) in accordance with the Projection Principle is actually (4):

(4) She told me [who]$_i$ she saw [NP$_i$ [e]$_i$].

This construction brings up a consequence of Move-Alpha and the Projection Principle: traces. Traces are phonetically empty copies of a moved item. The moved item and its trace are considered to be an abstract unit called a chain; this is the reason for the subscripts in (4) which relate *who* to its trace.

In addition to the above representational levels, the Government-Binding Theory is also an attempt to reduce the many constraints and rules found in natural language to a reduced set of universal principles which are more generally applicable to the languages of the world. In the sections which follow, each module of GB Theory will be briefly discussed in order to provide a background for the concepts used in this work.

1.1.2. X' Theory

X' Theory restricts the configuration of phrasal structures allowed in language. The restraints apply to D-structure where they pattern items from the lexicon in to phrases. The version of X' theory used in this work will be that of Chomsky (1986b). Lexical categories according to this theory are Verb, Noun, Preposition, and Adjective. The phrases which are at a higher level than these basic lexical categories are projected from them. Using 'X' as a symbol for all four lexical categories, the following equations show the basic framework of phrases:

(5) a. X' = X XP*
    b. XP = X' XP*

The asterisk indicates that such phrases can iterate. The order of elements depends on the language being used. This is where the previously mentioned parametric variation comes into play. If X, the head of a phrase, is on the left, the language is parameterized as a head-first language; if the head is on the right, the language is considered head-last. Languages such as English and Spanish have the parameter set for being head-first; Japanese is head-last.

The XP* on the right-hand side of X in (5a) is called a complement and the XP* on the right side of X in (5b) is referred to as a specifier. The examples in (6), from Baker (1988: 35), illustrate how X' theory constrains the representation of syntactic structure:

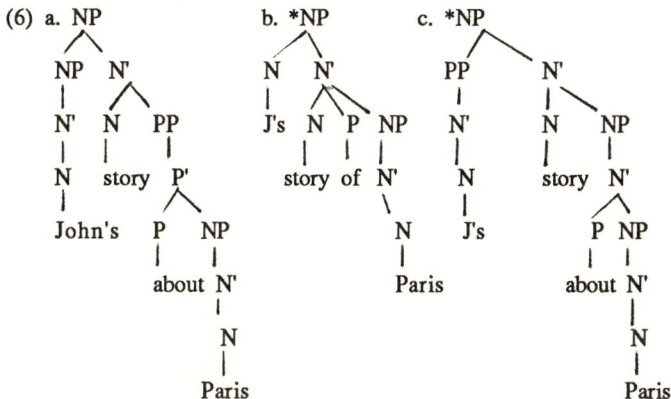

However, (6a) is the only well-formed representation. (6b) is not valid as it has nonmaximal phrases in the positions of complements and specifiers. (6c) is not a true representation of X' theory as it has phrases headed by the wrong kind of categories. Thus, these three structures illustrate the way in which X' theory limits linguistic structure.

Within X' theory, according to Chomsky (1986b), there are also two nonlexical categories, complementizer (C) and Infl (I) which are also considered heads as in (5). S, now known as IP, is the maximal projection of I; what was formerly called S' is now CP, the maximal projection of C. The subject of a clause is in the specifier of I' and the specifier of C' is the landing site for +wh elements such as *who* which was moved in example (4). The structure of a typical clause in English can be represented as in (7) (example from Baker 1988:36):

6   Lexical Categories in Spanish: The Determiner

(7)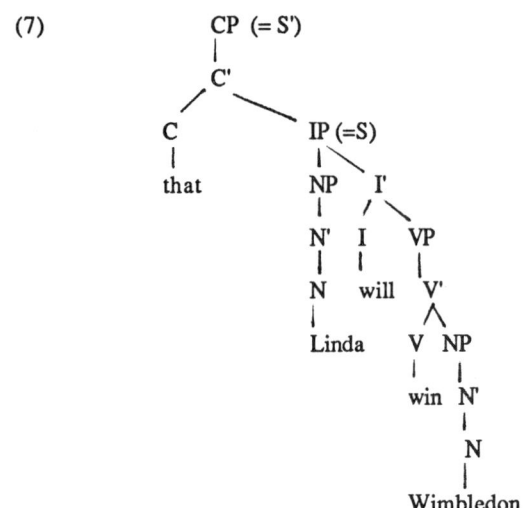

A notion related to X' theory is that of c-command. C-command is a basic structural relationship between a node and the projections it dominates. The formal definition can be found in (8):[1]

(8) A c-commands B iff A does not dominate B and for every maximal projection C, if C dominates A then C dominates B.

More simply put, c-command is a relation between two or more items in a tree, the higher item being able to c-command if it obeys the definition in (8). For example, in (6a) the NP *John's* c-commands the NP *Paris* but not vice versa. The NP *story* c-commands both *John's* and *Paris*. C-command will also be referred to as we examine other components of UG.

1.1.3. Theta (θ) Theory

Theta (θ) theory is a subcomponent of UG which is concerned with thematic relations in grammar. There are two types of θ roles which are assigned: external and internal. An internal θ role is assigned by a lexical head to its complement, whose structural depiction we saw in section 1.1.2. The external θ role is assigned compositionally by the head and its complements to the subject position (i.e. the specifier of I' or the specifier of N'). To illustrate, the verb *win* in (7) assigns its internal θ role to the NP *Wimbledon* and its external θ role to the subject of the clause *Linda*.

An important notion within θ theory is the Theta (θ) Criterion. As stated in Chomsky (1982), the θ-Criterion is defined as follows:

(9) Every term of LF that requires a theta role (each Argument) is associated with one and only one position to which theta roles are assigned, and each θ role determined by the lexical properties of a head is uniquely associated with one and only one argument.

Using lexical items to illustrate the θ-Criterion better shows its ability to constrain (examples from Baker (1988:37):

(10) a. I arrived.
 b. *I arrived a dog.
 c. I hit a dog.
 d. *I hit a dog a cat.

The intransitive verb *arrive* has one θ role which it assigns externally to *I*. That is why (10b) is ungrammatical; there is no θ role to assign to *a dog*. On the other hand, *hit* as a transitive verb has both an internal and external θ role to assign and in (10c) both of these roles are assigned. However, in (10d) there is an extra noun *cat* which receives no θ role and the sentence is therefore ungrammatical.

One more item which needs mentioning with regard to θ theory is that the θ-Criterion assumes that the θ role is assigned from one position to another. If an item is moved as a result of Move-Alpha, the θ role originally assigned is kept by the moved item and also retained by its trace. That is to say that the θ Criterion is applicable to the chain, not just the individual lexical item to which it was originally given.

1.1.4. Case Theory

The subcomponent of Case theory deals with the assignment of abstract Case to a category (usually an NP) that is governed by a lexical item able to assign Case. The lexical items able to assign Case are transitive verbs, prepositions, and tensed INFL. Using English as an example, a transitive verb assigns accusative Case to the object it governs, a preposition assigns oblique Case to its object, and a tensed INFL which governs the subject NP assigns it nominative Case. Although there is not much overt evidence in English for these Case assignments except in pronouns, Case is assumed to be assigned to all NPs to meet the Visibility Condition on LF (Chomsky (1986a) based on Aoun):

(11) An NP position which is the head of a chain (i.e. the last position of a moved category) can only have a θ index if it receives Case.

Because an NP normally will need a θ index, as explained in section 1.1.2, it will also need Case. The examples in (12) are grammatical and ungrammatical respectively due to Case or lack thereof:

(12) a. Mary INFL goes from house to house.
b. *Mary to go home.

In (12a), *Mary* receives nominative Case from the tensed INFL of the verb *goes*. The noun *house* is assigned oblique Case in the first instance by the preposition *from* and in the second instance by the preposition *to*. (12b) is ungrammatical because the infinitive *to go* is not tensed and therefore cannot assign nominative Case to *Mary*.

There are also two kinds of Case assignment- structural as we saw in (12), and inherent as with the English verb *to give*. As with X'-theory, Case assignment is subject to parametric variation among languages (i.e. rightward, leftward). For our purposes, we will be concerned with structural Case assignment in English and Spanish and the parametric variations these two languages may exhibit.

1.1.5. Government

Government involves the relations between the location of two items in a phrase or sentence. The formal definition of Government according to Chomsky (1986b:9) is as follows:

(13) α governs β iff α m-commands β and there is no γ, such that γ a barrier for β, such that γ excludes α.

As we saw in section 1.1.2, c-command means that A is higher in the tree than B and they are close enough to each other that no intervening category C contains B but not A. The Chomsky (1986b) definition of *barrier* is quite technical so for our purposes we will assume that all and only maximal categories except for IP are barriers. (Aoun and Sportiche (1983)). Another consideration with regard to barriers is that they are relative to the individual positions of the elements involved. Using (6) as an example, PP is a barrier between *story* and *Paris* but *story* can govern *John's* because there are no barriers. In (7), *win* can govern *Wimbledon* but not *Linda* as *Linda* is not c-commanded by the verb.

One important principle directly related to government is the Empty Category Principle (ECP). Because we will deal more extensively with the ECP in Chapter Three, we will only mention it briefly here. The ECP as formulated by Chomsky (1981) states:

(14) All empty categories must be properly governed.

Empty categories include traces and other phonetically null categories such as pro and variables. The ECP is especially useful with regard to Move-Alpha and will be applied in Spanish to empty nominals discussed in Chapter Three.

1.1.6. Binding Theory

This subcomponent of UG concerns the relationship of pronouns and anaphors with their antecedents. There are three Principles which are specified by the Binding theory and they are summarized in (15):

(15) Principle A: Anaphors (reflexive and reciprocal expressions) must be bound in their governing category.
Principle B. Pronouns must be free in their governing category.
Principle C: Referential (R) expressions be free.

The definition of binding is that A binds B iff A c-commands B and A and B are coindexed. The coindexation is a necessary result of B depending on A for reference.

The notion of governing category is one of local relations. A category which has both a subject in the sense of X' and an item that governs the element in question is enough to provide a governing category. The sentences in (16) will illustrate the principles of the Binding theory (examples from Baker (1988:42)):

(16) a. Mark thinks that [Sara$_i$ likes herself$_i$].
    *Sara$_i$ thinks that [Mark$_i$ likes herself$_i$].
b. *Mark thinks that [Sara$_i$ likes her$_i$].
    Sara$_i$ thinks that [Mark likes her$_i$].
c. *Mark thinks that [she$_i$ likes Sara$_i$].
    *She$_i$ thinks that [Mark likes Sara$_i$].

These sentences show that anaphors such as *herself* in (16a) need to have an antecedent very near, pronouns such as *her* in (16b) cannot have an antecedent which is close, and R-expressions such as names may not have antecedents as seen in (16c). Traces such as those left by a +wh element which moved are subject to Principle C of the Binding theory. Traces left by the movement of an NP are subject to Principle

A and act as though they were anaphors. The empty pronoun pro which is found in languages like Spanish obeys Principle B just like those pronouns which are overt.

In addition to pro, there is also an empty pronoun referred to in the GB theory as PRO. PRO is considered to be both a pronoun and an anaphor. Since PRO is subject to both Principle A and B of the Binding theory and these principles contradict each other, PRO is always considered to be ungoverned, having no governing category. For the most part, the only ungoverned position in English is the subject of an infinitive and that is where we find PRO:

(17) a. You$_i$ need [PRO$_i$ to go to sleep].
    b. *You$_i$ need [the president to play golf PRO$_i$].
    c. *You$_i$ hope [PRO$_i$ will see the president].

In (17a), PRO is the subject of an infinitive and is ungoverned so the sentence is grammatical. In (17b), the verb *to play* governs PRO and it is governed in (17c) by the INFL of the tensed verb *will*. Whenever PRO is in a governed setting, the resulting sentence will always be ungrammatical. We will refer again to PRO and the Principles of the Binding theory in Chapter Three.

1.1.7. Control Theory

Control theory is related to Binding theory in that it is concerned with coreference. It specifies the referent of PRO. PRO, as we saw in 1.1.6, can never be in a position where it is governed, however, it can be interpreted as referring to a particular antecedent. If PRO has no antecedent, it is said to be uncontrolled; if it has a referent, it is said to be controlled. (18) shows an example of uncontrolled and controlled PRO, respectively:

(18) a. PRO To live in New York is a great experience.
    b. I$_i$ want [PRO$_i$ to live in New York].

In this work, control theory will not play a great role and therefore we will not elaborate further on this subcomponent of UG.

1.1.8. Conclusions

We have now briefly reviewed the Government-Binding theory and its subcomponents which are relevant to the discussion of determiner phrases which follows. There are other modules of GB and other universals which have not been discussed in this chapter due to their lack of pertinence to the topic at hand. However, it should be clear at this point that the GB theory has and continues to undergo changes, modifications, and refinements. With so many interacting principles and variations of definitions, it is hoped that this chapter will be able to supply the reader with the basic theoretical assumptions and definitions necessary to understand the chapters which follow.

1.2. Overview

In the work that follows, I will provide evidence that the determiner is a lexical category. Chapter Two will provide background information about the DP hypothesis and previous theoretical assumptions concerning lexical and functional categories. Chapter Three deals with the similarities and differences between Spanish and English determiner phrases headed by a definite article or demonstrative. Of special interest are the empty nominal phrases headed by a determiner which occur in Spanish but not in English. Chapter Four treats the possessive/genitive construction in Spanish and English. I argue that treatment of the determiner as a lexical head eliminates the need for intermediate phrases proposed in previous studies (Mallén 1988).

NOTES TO CHAPTER 1

[1] Chomsky (1986b) calls this m-command to differentiate it from another notion of c-command in which all the categories that contain the element which commands to also contain the commanded elements. But the definition in (8) is applicable to our discussion.

Chapter 2

General Theoretical Assumptions About Determiner Phrases

2.0. INTRODUCTION

An important constituent when speaking of syntactic categories is the determiner phrase (DP), formerly referred to as 'Noun Phrase' or NP. The term DP, first used by Brame (1981) within the framework of lexically based syntax, is founded upon the notion that the head of the phrase is a determiner. Determiners are a closed class of items that are grammatically known as articles, demonstrative adjectives, possessive adjectives, and numerals. Their presence is at times optional in both Spanish and English as seen in the following examples:

(1) a. Muchas veces me daba *flores*.
'Many times he gave me *flowers*.'
b. Muchas veces me daba *flores del jardín*.
'Many times he gave me *flowers from the garden*.'
c. Muchas veces me daba *unas flores*.
'Many times he gave me *some flowers*.'
d. Muchas veces me daba *unas flores del jardín*.
'Many times he gave me *some flowers from the garden*.'

In (1a) the determiner and complement positions are absent, in (1b) the determiner of *flores* is empty but there is a modifier *del jardín* present. (1c) has a filled determiner but no modifying prepositional phrase and (1d) has both a determiner and modifier.

In the examples in (1), the italicized phrases are in object position and therefore are able to vary with respect to determiner usage. The rules regarding determiners preceding a noun in subject position are more stringent in Spanish than in English:

(2) *Flores son hermosas.
     'Flowers are beautiful.'

In Spanish, a noun filling the role of subject of the sentence must be preceded by a determiner in order to be acceptable but in English this is not the case.[1] A sentence such as (2) is grammatical either with or without a determiner as shown by the English gloss for (2). The requirements for determiner usage with a subject in English are therefore different than in Spanish.

Another structural requirement in Spanish that English does not have is the use of a determiner in a noun phrase in which the noun has been deleted. In fact, this construction, with or without determiner, is not permitted in English:

(3) a. Quiero las de Jaime.
       *'I want the (fem. plural) of Jaime.'
    b. *Quiero de Jaime.
       *'I want of Jaime.'

The structural make-up of DPs such as (3) and other similar constructions will be examined in more detail in Chapter 3 but first it is important to establish the current theoretical status of DPs. In section 2.1, I review the DP hypothesis of Abney (1987). In the same section, we will discuss the motivation for the DP hypothesis and the similarities and differences between NPs and sentences which are related to the hypothesis. Also included in the section will be the structure which Abney proposes for the DP, the characteristics of functional and thematic categories and a discussion of PRO in NP. The expansion of Abney's proposal by Fukui and Speas (1986) and their movement hypothesis regarding the assignment of Kase by functional categories will be the topic in section 2.2. In section 2.3, I will critique both Abney and Fukui and Speas since their proposals are related. In section 2.4, I will develop my own hypothesis for the Spanish determiner as a lexical category and section 2.5 will summarize the findings of this chapter.

2.1. ABNEY'S DP HYPOTHESIS

In this section, we will review the evidence for the determiner phrase (DP) hypothesis as proposed by Abney (1987). The reasons for the hypothesis, the similarities and differences between clauses and noun phrases, and the structure of DPs will be discussed. In addition to the previously mentioned concerns, the distinction between functional and lexical categories as proposed by Abney will be summarized.

2.1.1. Motivation for the DP Hypothesis

Abney has several reasons for proposing that the determiner is the head of its phrase. First, when determiners are found alone, they have every indication and behavior of a noun phrase which, in Abney's opinion, would not be expected unless the phrase they project is a noun phrase. A second reason is that standard NP analysis does not provide enough positions to account for all the types of elements that can appear pre-nominally in a phrase; the DP analysis gives the extra specifier positions necessary while adhering to a two-bar X-bar theory. Finally the major reason for positing a determiner-as-head analysis is Abney's quest to find a clause-like structure for the noun phrase or as he calls it, the determiner phrase, and has led to what is now known as the DP hypothesis. Nouns which show agreement with their possessors according to Abney must have some type of Infl position which heads the phrase and provides the Agr element. The following examples from Abney illustrate the standard possessor NP in (4a) versus the type of DP structure he proposes for the possessor in (4b):

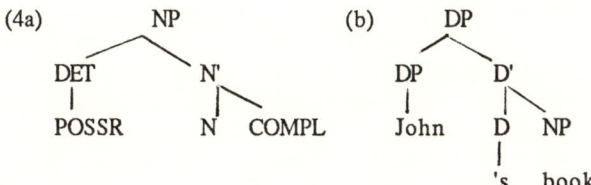

He calls that head position of the NP 'D' and claims that a determiner filling D is the lexical realization of D just as a modal verb is the lexical realization of Infl. Both the noun phrase and the clause have inflectional elements which in the case of the NP will take a projection of N and in that of the clause, takes a projection of V.

Whereas in the VP the modal expresses the inflection of the verb, the nominal equivalent is the determiner. The structures he proposes for English DPs are seen here in (5):

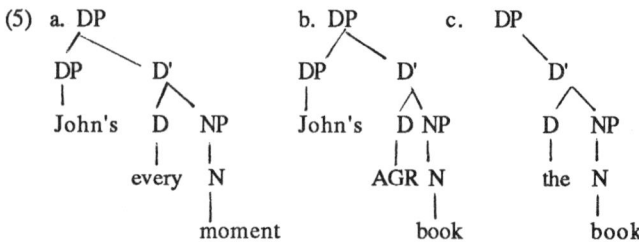

However, after proposing the structures above, Abney poses two questions: Does an Infl head of a noun phrase really exist? and is D which he calls the mystery category equal to Determiner? It is certainly desirable to propose a sentence-like structure for the NP (or DP) since the noun and verb are the most important parts of every sentence and a similar structure for both would perhaps account for easier acquisition by children. But, even Abney himself admits that there are some important differences between the sentence and the noun phrase although these disparities are not enough to cause him to abandon the DP analysis. His primary concern is that of finding an Infl-type element which serves as head of a noun phrase.

2.1.2. Similarities Between Noun Phrases and Sentences

The similarities Abney mentions between noun phrases and sentences include the ability of both to function as either subject or direct object of a sentence and the ability to be passivized, properties which were first noted by Lees (1960). The examples from Abney given below illustrate these properties:

(6) a. *John* surprised me.
 That John came surprised me.
 b. I know *John*.
 I know *that John came*.
 c. *John* was known *t* by many linguists.
 That John came was known *t* by many linguists.

Because of these similarities, Abney says that Lees predicted that embedded sentences would be dominated by an NP node. For Lees, a nominalization was any structure that had internal semantics which were sentence-like. A derived nominal such as (7) would be produced by a transformation applied to a sentence in order to account for the synonymy of both structures:

(7) a. [Nero's destruction of Rome] dismayed the Senate.
  b. [That Nero destroyed Rome] dismayed the Senate.
  (examples from Abney 1987:32)

Lees' definition of nominalization included gerunds, derived nominals and any category which occurred in argument position. Abney states that this was a commonly held early generativist viewpoint; embedded sentences could be dominated by an NP or even a noun head which was deleted before S-structure. A non-transformational approach introduced by Chomsky (1970) recognized that there is a structural necessity for subject/object distinction for both sentences and noun phrases and X-bar theory with its N-bar node was born of that need. The differences in Case and theta assignment for subject sentences versus subject noun phrases as well as thematic similarities between the two were, of course, noted later by Chomsky (1981). For example, both sentences and NPs are subject to the same binding and control restrictions, seen respectively in (8) and (9):

(8) a. John$_i$ portrayed himself$_i$.
    John$_i$'s portrayal of himself$_i$.
  b. *himself$_i$ portrayed John$_i$/him$_i$.
    *his own portrayal of John$_i$/him$_i$.
  c. John recommended for [himself$_i$ to portray himself$_i$.]
    John recommended [his own$_i$ portrayal of himself$_i$.]
  d. *John recommended for [himself$_i$ to portray him$_i$.]
    *John recommended [his own$_i$ portrayal of him$_i$.]

(9) a. John criticized Bill$_j$ after his$_j$ talk.
    John's criticism of Bill$_j$ after his$_j$ talk.

b. *John criticized Bill$_j$ after PRO$_j$ talking.
 *John's criticism of Bill$_j$ after PRO$_j$ talking.
 (examples from Abney 1987:33)

Although the notion that NPs are derived from their verbal counterparts by transformations is no longer supported in current linguistic theory, the similarities between clauses and noun phrases are enough for Abney to maintain his DP hypothesis and continue his search for a sentence-like structure for DPs.

2.1.3. Differences Between Noun Phrases and Sentences

Although Abney's arguments in favor of the DP and sentence having a similar structure seem convincing, there are still many differences between the two categories. A major contrast is the apparent lack of predication in noun phrases. Since only maximal categories are able to be syntactic predicates and N-bar is a non-maximal category, Abney's argument is that there is a lack of predication in N-bar. However, the kind of predication Abney suggests for N-bar versus sentence is that of semantic, not syntactic predication. For example, the NP *destruction of the city* is parallel in meaning to the VP *destroy the city* which illustrates that predication of a syntactic nature is not at issue here.

Another difference between sentence and noun phrase is the optional nature of the subject in NP but its requirement in a sentence. A pleonastic subject must be inserted in a sentence but never in an NP:

(10) a. there arrived a man
 b. *there's arrival of a man
 c. It was decided that he should leave
 d. *its decision that he should leave

There are further specific restrictions on NP constructions which are unlike those found in a sentence. Restrictions on passivization, the absence of an object with psych nouns, the inability to raise to subject or object position, the impossibility of reduced clause complements, lack of *tough* or object control constructions, lack of resultative secondary predicates or object pleonastics, and absence of indirect or concealed questions are all restrictions that differentiate noun phrases from clauses. All of these very specific differences between NP and sentence are discussed in detail but are considered secondary differences in comparison to the three main differences of verbs versus nouns: only verbs can have oblique arguments, take reduced clauses as a complement, and can undergo incorporation. Since, however, the above differences deal with complements, not specifiers, Abney's DP analysis is not affected and he cites selectional differences rather than structural ones as the reason for the dichotomy between nouns and verbs. Ultimately, he would like to combine the three main differences listed above into one all-encompassing difference and he does so under the notion of incorporation. The verb can experience incorporation but a noun cannot.

A further difference between nouns and verbs is that since nouns cannot assign Case to their objects, unlike a verb, a noun cannot have an NP complement:

(11) The enemy destroyed the city
 *The enemy's destruction the city

Normally, the insertion of the preposition *of* before the NP occurs in order to produce a grammatical utterance. As is standard, Abney explains this *of* as a case assigner much like possessive *'s* but he distinguishes between the two by calling *'s* a genitive Case assigner and *of* a partitive Case assigner. He cautions that what he means by partitive is merely the case marked by *of*, not a partitive in the general sense of the word. The noun is said to assign partitive case and D_{AGR} is the element that assigns genitive Case. Either one of these case assigners can head a Kase phrase (KP) which is in object position. Kase is a term used to encompass both the Case assigned by lexical categories and that which is assigned by functional categories such as *'s*. The case the object is actually assigned must agree with the case marked which requires raising to a position of genitive case assignment if the noun shows genitive marking. The example from Abney in (5) renumbered as (12) illustrates the genitive Case assignment in DP, however, the partitive *of* construction is not shown in Abney's work:

(12)
```
        DP
       /  \
      DP   D'
      |   /  \
    John's D  NP
           |  |
          AGR N
              |
             book
```

2.1.4. The Structure of DP

Abney's next task is to show where his proposed functional element, the determiner, will appear in NP structure. The standard analysis is found in (13):

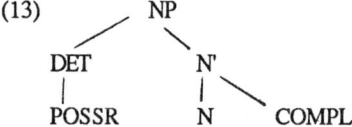

(13)
```
        NP
       /  \
     DET   N'
      |   / \
    POSSR N  COMPL
```

Since determiners only occur in noun phrases (with some exceptions)[2] and nouns frequently need a determiner, the structure of DP must reflect this relationship. After examining various structures, Abney argues that D is the head of NP, renamed DP, and chooses a projection of N as its complement:

(14)
```
      DetP
      / \
    Det  NP
         |
         N
```

Abney's arguments for the structure in (14) are the following: the opportunity to group Det with other functional categories, an ability to have NPs conform to X' theory, and additional specifier positions which better capture the structure of natural language. A further claim, that Det has all the properties of a functional category, will be outlined in the next section when functional versus lexical category properties will be detailed. He argues that an advantage of this analysis of DP lies in its capacity to group Det with the functional categories COMP and Infl as well as the ability to consider non-thematic categories as perfectly in line with X bar theory since Det is the head of its phrase. Finally, Abney observes that in the Det-as-head analysis there is no need to assume that determiner and possessor appear in the same place in a phrase. This can be seen by the addition of an extra spec position since DP as well as NP each have a Spec (below labeled as 1 and 2):

(15)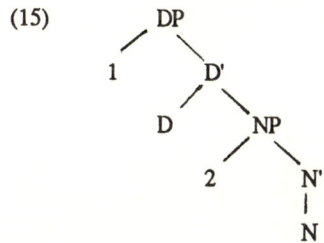

A further argument for (14) derives from assumptions of X'-Theory proposed in Stowell (1981) and later expanded upon in Chomsky (1986b). The proposal is made that there are X^0 positions and X^{max} positions in language which are in complementary distribution with each other. A position such as Spec or a complement position can only be filled with maximal projections, not X^0s. In the same way, an X^{max} cannot fill an X^0 slot. Abney claims that this strong version of X bar theory allows us to adopt the Det-as-head analysis without having to worry about why DetP is never filled with anything but a Det.

The Det-as-head analysis also provides a symmetry between the functional and thematic categories as illustrated in (16).

(16) [$_{CP}$ what [$_{IP}$ Julia played t]]
 [$_{IP}$ the violin [$_{VP}$ was played t]]
 [$_{DP}$ the city's [$_{NP}$ destruction t]]

Only functional categories characteristically have overt subjects and by assuming that only functional categories contain AGR, it can also be assumed that only the subject position of functional categories is available for movement by substitution.

Abney says that another advantage of the parallel analysis of Infl and Det lies in their semantic relatedness. Infl, by locating or determining the tense of VP does the same thing for the verb that the determiner does for the noun- it picks out a particular item within the extension of the noun.

2.1.5. Functional versus Thematic Elements

In this section, we will discuss the distinction first proposed by Abney that language has both functional and lexical categories. The distinction is important with regard to determiners because Abney classifies them as functional elements along with INFL and COMP. The consequences of this dichotomy in language will be examined below.

For Abney, Infl is representative of the class of elements he calls functional elements which contrast with thematic elements such as verbs, nouns, and adjectives. There is no doubt that functional elements can have lexical realization like any lexical entry in language, however, he claims that functional categories have certain characteristics in common which are opposed to those of thematic elements. The most important quality is the property of selecting a unique complement which is neither an argument nor adjunct of the functional category. For the two commonly accepted functional categories, Comp and Infl, C chooses the complement IP and I chooses VP. Each category chooses a unique complement and unlike the lexical categories, the complement is not a distinct object from C or I. That is to say, in a phrase such as *That Julia played the violin*, the VP *played the violin*, the IP *Julia played the violin*, and the CP *that Julia played the violin* all semantically depict the action of playing the violin.

A thematic head such as the NP *the violin*, on the other hand, describes a violin and when serving as the complement of a verb such as *played*, the VP does not merely describe a violin but rather depicts the action of playing the violin. Abney claims that this difference in relation between a head and its complement is due to the nature of thematic versus functional selection. The syntactic relationship between a functional head and its complement he calls f-selection. F-selection is the ability of the complement to pass its descriptive content on to the head of the phrase. Thematic elements, those complements which do not pass their descriptive content on to the head of the phrase are classified as [-F] as opposed to the functional elements which are [+F].

Abney does acknowledge that the definitive properties for functional elements do not necessarily have neat boundary lines; there are atypical elements within every grammatical category. Nevertheless, he suggests that the classes remain [± F] although it is sometimes difficult to know how to classify a particular element. Of course, the head of the NP is for him the [+F] category D which in contrast to the [+F] categories Infl and Comp is nominal, not verbal. Furthermore, while the [± N], [± V] division is important, there are many more syntactic categories in language than N, V, A, and P, including Adv, Q, Conj, Det, Infl, and Comp. Because of these additional categories, Abney chooses to use the distinction [± F], [± N] to delineate the four major syntactic categories. These are summarized in (17):

(17)   [-F]   [+F]
       [-N]   V, Aux, P   I, C
       [+N]   N, A, Q, Adv   D

Of course, even these divisions do not cover categories like conjunctions which Abney says are [+F] but unspecified for [± N]. In the same way, P seems to be unspecified for [± F]; it seems to play an intermediate role between thematic and functional.

Abney cites additional support for the above dichotomy going back to the *Poetics* of Aristotle and the 19th century Japanese grammarian Suzuki who divided language into the four categories noun, verb, adjective, and particle (case markers, modals, etc.). He cites as further evidence that children acquire functional elements later than thematic ones and in certain aphasias, the ability to understand thematic elements remains undamaged while the ability to use functional elements is lost. Although some items are hard to categorize as there are some thematic elements which have some properties of functional elements and vice versa, Abney says this should not cancel out the division between the two classes.

The characteristics of functional categories according to Abney are as follows:

(18) a. Functional categories are a closed class; they do not admit new members.
     b. Functional categories have only one complement which is not usually an argument. Arguments are CP, PP, and DP. Functional elements do not select these but rather select for IP, NP, and VP.
     c. Functional elements are generally dependent morphological and phonological items. They are generally not stressed, often are clitics or affixes, and at times, are phonologically null.
     d. Functional elements are usually unable to be separated from their complement.
     e. Functional category members do not have the independent descriptive ability attributed to thematic category members. That is to say, the meaning of a functional category makes a contribution to the meaning of its complement; it marks a

grammatical relation or relational feature instead of specifying one of a class of objects.

f. A final point which Abney says is crucial is that traditional grammarians such as Aristotle and Suzuki have noted that there is a difference between functional and thematic elements in language. Aristotle defines functional elements as 'words without meaning' in contrast to thematic ones which he calls 'words with meaning'. Suzuki, in a similar vein, says that functional elements denote nothing while thematic elements denote something.[3] Abney claims that Functional elements lack the descriptive substance of thematic elements. For example, if a thematic element like *book* or *read* is uttered in isolation, some object or action is described. On the other hand, if the same thing occurs with a functional element like *the*, there is no meaning to the element in isolation.

Unlike C and I, the other functional categories, however, Abney states that 'D does not seem to be selected by a matrix head, and as is well known, selectional restrictions *are* imposed on N.' (Abney 1987:85). This would seem to argue against the idea of D as the head of a phrase but since the restrictions on N are of a semantic, not a syntactic sort this is not as problematic as it would seem. The subcategorization that imposes selectional restrictions on a noun in the lexicon will apply to that noun whether it is in subject or object position. For instance, the N that is found with a verb such as *fear* or *frighten* must be an animate one (examples from Abney 1987:86):

(19) a. Sincerity frightens John.
 b. *John frightens sincerity.
 c. *Sincerity fears John.
 d. John fears sincerity.

It should be noted that the verb which imposes the restriction does not govern the subject. Therefore, even though it is still a mystery why verbs do not select for particular determiners it is just as puzzling that verbs do not select for any part of the noun phrase like they do for C and I.

2.1.6. PRO in NP (DP)

Another problem seemingly solved with the proposal of the DP analysis is the question of PRO in NP. Previously, this was not possible without changing some assumptions about PRO's governability. For example, under standard analysis, PRO could never be found in the subject position of a noun phrase because the noun phrase was the maximal projection of N and therefore, its subject position was always governed. PRO, due to its binding theory properties, cannot be found in a governed position. But in the DP analysis, PRO is allowed in the subject position because D, not being lexical, may not be a governor, although if there is an external governor or if DP is a barrier this status may change. In sentences such as (20a) that have an implicit agent as proposed by Roeper (1984), the appearance of PRO in subject position is illustrated:

(20) a. the PRO review of the book [PRO to prove a point]
b. *the book's review [PRO to prove a point]

This does not mean that a PRO must be present in every DP, simply that if there is no possessor theta role assigned by D (when there is no *'s* present in the phrase) then PRO can be a subject of DP. One argument in favor of this is the θ theory assumption that a derived action nominal like *destruction* has an external θ-role to assign and will assign it to PRO as the agent of *destruction*:

(21) [$_{DP}$ PRO the [$_{NP}$ destruction of the city]]

Abney assumes that the NP assigns its θ role to PRO by means of predication in (21) but when a possessor agent is present as in (22), the possessor is assigned Case by D$_{AGR}$ but gets its θ-role from NP:

(22) [$_{DP}$ Caesar's [$_{NP}$ destruction of the city]]

As a result of his study, Abney maintains that there is a dichotomy in language between nominal and verbal elements and between functional and thematic ones. His claim of D as the head of its phrase will be adopted in this work. However, the hypothesis that D is a functional category and not a lexical one will be examined in light of Spanish data.

2.2. ANALYSIS OF FUKUI AND SPEAS (1986)

An approach which builds on Abney's proposal is the Fukui and Speas (1986) study of the structure of functional categories. In this section, we will review their proposal as it pertains to English.

A linguistic convention used since Chomsky (1970), is the division of the parts of speech into the groups $\pm$N and $\pm$V. Fukui and Speas begin their discussion with a review of these divisions. The following lexical categories are derived: nouns, adjectives, verbs, and prepositions. These are illustrated in (23):

(23) a. +N -V = noun
b. +N +V = adjective
c. -N -V = verb
d. -N -V = preposition

The four lexical categories depicted by these features are the only ones which may take an argument and contain a theta grid as part of their lexical make-up. This contrasts with the functional categories, which cannot. But in Spanish, as well as in English, there is an additional type of category necessary to capture the structure of well-formed sentences. Categories such as INFL and COMP are called functional categories and head their own phrases as seen in (24):

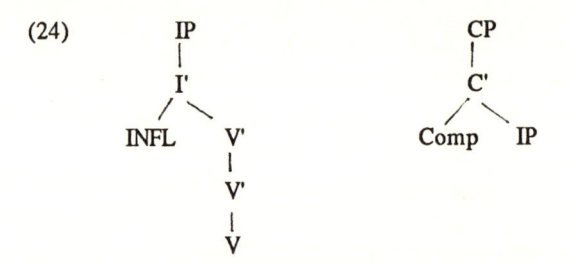

(24)
```
        IP                    CP
        |                     |
        I'                    C'
       / \                   / \
    INFL  V'              Comp  IP
          |
          V'
          |
          V
```

However, since INFL and COMP are not actual lexical items, they must be classified according to different features. Instead of calling these categories non-lexical, Fukui and Speas (1986) refer to them as Functional categories. The Functional categories, according to Fukui and Speas, differ from lexical ones in that the Functional category is said to have a unique specifier position which closes off its projection. That is to say, there is only one specifier position available for functional categories and by closing off the projection, the specifier no longer allows any iteration of the category. Thus, the node which dominates the functional category's projection is X" (XP) whereas the lexical category may iterate specifiers dominated by X'.[4] A specifier is the term used for the immediate daughter of any X" category. Categories such as adverbs, adjectives, and verbs are able to have more than one specifier filled with the same type of lexical item as seen in the following Fukui and Speas examples:

(25) a. the very very old man
 b. Mary's big red book
 c. Susan never could have been eating cabbage

Structurally, an example such as (25a) can be illustrated by (26) which depicts the iteration of specifiers:

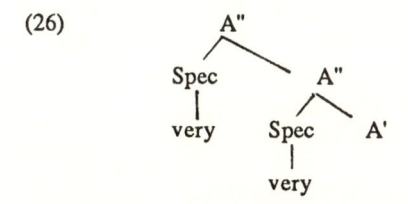

(26)
```
        A"
       /  \
     Spec   A"
      |    /  \
     very Spec  A'
           |
          very
```

On the other hand, Fukui and Speas use the examples in (27) to support their theory that determiners, because of their status as a Functional category, cannot iterate:

(27) a. *the the old man
 b. *the John's cat

The structure in (28) would be applicable to an example like *the old man*:

(28)
```
            DP
            |
            D'
           / \
         DET  N'
          |   |
         the (DP)
              |
              N'
             / \
            N  (DP)
            |
            man
```

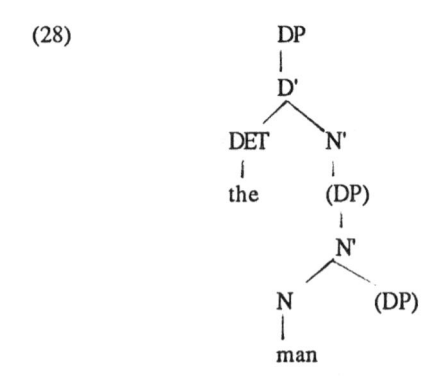

For now, we can assume that the examples in (27) are ungrammatical because they have more than one determiner, a functional category which does not iterate. This assumption allows the proposed structure of DPs to be parallel to that of the functional category phrases CP and IP.

2.2.1. Properties of Functional Categories

Certain properties in addition to the unique specifier position characterize functional categories according to Fukui and Speas. First, lexical heads may govern and Kase mark into their complements, functional heads cannot. However, no examples of these properties are provided in the Fukui and Speas work. This ability to govern and Kase mark is due to directionality since a lexical category governs to the right in a head-initial language, while a functional category governs to its left. As we noted in Section 2.2.3, Kase is the term used to denote the assignment of both lexical and functional Case. The specifier of a functional head is moved from within its complement and every functional head may have a specifier (Spec) position. The Spec position of a functional category must be Kase marked in order to be allowed in a representation; otherwise the category's projection will be X' instead of X".[5] The functional head itself may provide the Kase assignment to the Spec position (licensing by F-feature) or a lexical element can provide Kase assignment for such items as Exceptional Case Marking verbs like *believe*.

Second, functional categories are also said to be closed classes, that is, they do not allow new additions like lexical categories do and lack the semantic richness of lexical category members. These two points as well as the notion that functional heads always select a unique complement are credited to Abney (1986).

Each functional category has some members which are able to assign Function features (F-features) and others which do not have this ability. As an example of F-feature assignment, Fukui and Speas mention nominative case, which is assigned by tense/agreement features, *'s*, which assigns genitive case in English, and +Wh given by a Wh Comp as examples of F-features. The example in (29) from Fukui and Speas shows genitive case assignment by the functional category DET:

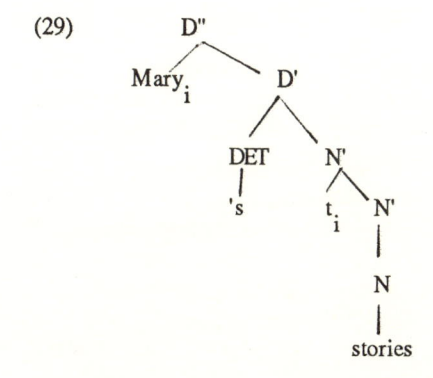

(29)
```
         D"
        /  \
     Mary   D'
        i  / \
         DET  N'
          |  / \
         's t   N'
             i  |
                N
                |
              stories
```

F-features in addition to the lexical Case assigners Verb ([+V -N]) and Preposition ([-V -N]) are given a more general heading of Kase in order to generalize across lexically and functionally assigned Case. Kase markers of the Spec position are normally Functional heads (Comp, Infl, or Det). However, the Spec of IP can be Kase-marked by exceptional case-marking verbs, through the lexical marking of Case.

2.2.2. Movement

Another consideration which a movement analysis entails is the question of unique specifiers for Functional categories. Since in the Fukui and Speas proposal the only items which are found in this position have moved there at S-structure, the landing site is thought to be one of adjunction which forms a barrier when an item moves there to receive its F-features, thus precluding further movement. The spec of a Functional category is only optionally present in a phrase and is licensed by Universal Grammar which is operative at D-structure, not 'by well-formedness conditions on phrase markers' (Fukui and Speas 1986:130). An argument that Fukui and Speas present for the uniqueness of Functional category specifiers is that Universal Grammar has no counting mechanisms and these F-categories which serve to link parts of a sentence, are found in 'construction with only 2 constituents of the sentence in any given structure, hence its unique spec (and unique complement)' (Fukui and Speas 1986:145). If Kase is given to the spec of X', then and only then can X' project to X". Therefore, the only 'truly empty' positions at D-structure are those licensed by Kase; specs of F-categories are no exception. These specs are empty because Kase assignment is accomplished at S-structure but theta assignment is at D-structure. Theta-assignment is given only inside the phrasal projection of a Lexical head.

As in Chomsky (1986b), A directly theta marks B iff A and B are sisters. That means A and B mutually c-command each other. L-marking is a 'subset' of direct theta marking. A L- marks B iff A is a *lexical* head which directly θ-marks B. Functional heads do not possess the ability to theta mark because they lack theta grids. Structurally, this inability to θ-mark becomes crucial when dealing with extraction out of DPs.

For Fukui and Speas there is very little difference between phrases like (30) which contain a complex DP and those like (31) which have a relative clause until one tries to extract from out of either structure, as demonstrated in (32) and (33):

(30) [$_{D'}$the[$_{N'}$claim[$_{C''}$that[$_{I''}$Mary[$_{I'}$[$_{V'}$likes Bill]]]]]]
(31) [$_{D'}$the[$_{N'}$man[$_{C''}$who$_i$[$_{C'}$[$_{I''}$Mary[$_{I'}$[$_{V'}$likes t$_i$]]]]]]]
(32) *Who do you believe the claim that Mary likes t
(33) **Who did you see the woman who likes t

The ungrammaticality in (32) is due to the fact that nouns like *claim* do not subcategorize for a WH element which would license the spec position of their complement through Kase. As we saw previously, a Functional category only projects to X' when no Kase is assigned to its Spec. Thus, the complement of *claim* is C' and extraction out of it poses a subjacency violation because of the crossing of I" which is a barrier. Extraction out of the relative clause in (33) is even worse because the clause has a COMP which projects to C" due to its Wh element (which has Kase) and extraction out of it crosses two barriers (I" and C"). Similar ungrammaticality occurs when extraction from a complex DP with a subject like (34) is compared to the subjectless complex DP (33) renumbered as (35):

(34) **Who do you believe Susan's claim that Mary likes?
(35) *Who do you believe the claim that Mary likes?

In (35), *the claim that Mary likes* only projects to D' because *the* has no F-features to assign, thus there is no spec as a sister to D' and only one barrier is crossed. However, in (34), *Susan* has moved to the spec of DP in order to receive the Kase that the F-feature *'s* has to assign. Since the maximal category of (34) is D", two barriers, D" and C" are crossed which makes (34) less grammatical than (35).

2.3. CRITIQUE OF ABNEY AND FUKUI AND SPEAS

In this section we will see if the previously reviewed analyses of Abney and Fukui and Speas sufficiently account for the determiner phrase in Spanish.

2.3.1. Critique of Abney

Beginning with Abney's proposal of the DP hypothesis, we will critique his work especially in light of his categorization of the determiner as a functional category.

2.3.2. Discussion of Abney with regard to Spanish

Abney's proposal that the determiner is the head of its own phrasal category will be assumed to be correct. His detailed study of English and Hungarian among other languages seems to point to a similar structure for both sentences and noun phrases within the configuration of X' theory. With respect to Spanish, we will assume that D is the head of its phrase. However, Abney's structure in (5b) for the genitive phrase in English will not be applicable to Spanish since Spanish does not assign genitive Case by means of an *'s*. My proposal for Spanish will be found in section 2.4.

Abney mentions that both clauses and noun phrases have the properties of passivization and the ability to serve either as subject or direct object in a structure. These properties are also true of Spanish sentences and NPs:

(36) a. *Julia* me asustó. '*Julia* frightened me.'
Que Julia llegó me asustó. '
That Julia arrived frightened me.'
b. *Julia* fue admirada por mucha gente. '
Julia was admired by many people.'
Que Julia llegó fue admirado por mucha gente.
'*That Julia arrived* was admired by many people.'
La destrucción de la ciudad nos asustó.
'The destruction of the city frightened us.'
c. *Que la ciudad fue destruída* nos asustó.
'That the city was destroyed frightened us.'

Also in Spanish as well as in English, clauses and noun phrases behave similarly with respect to control and binding as can be seen in (37) and (38) respectively:

(37) a. Julia$_i$ se$_i$ pintó. 'Julia$_i$ painted herself$_i$.'
b. la pintura de Julia$_i$ por sí misma$_i$. 'Julia's$_i$ painting of herself$_i$.'
c. Julia se$_i$ recomendó pintarse$_i$. 'Julia recommended that she$_i$ paint herself$_i$.'
d. Julia recomendó su propia pintura$_i$ de sí misma$_i$.
'Julia recommended her own$_i$ painting of herself$_i$.'

(38) a. Julio alabó a Juan$_j$ después de su$_j$ acción.
'Julio praised John$_j$ after his$_j$ action.'
b. La alabanza de Julio a Juan$_j$ después de su$_j$ acción.
'Julio's praise of Juan$_j$ after his$_j$ action.'
c. *Julio alabó a Juan$_j$ después de PRO$_j$ actuar.
*'Julio praised Juan$_j$ after PRO$_j$ acting.'
d. *La alabanza de Julio a Juan$_j$ después de PRO$_j$ actuar.
'*Julio's praise of Juan$_j$ after PRO$_j$ acting.'

(In (38 c and d), the sentences are grammatical if *Julio* is coindexed with and controls PRO.)

Even so, it is well known that just because two categories can be found in similar environments does not imply that they are one and the same category. In spite of the similarities between English and Spanish noted above, there are differences between the DPs in the two languages. These will be discussed in section 2.3.4.

2.3.3. Discussion of Functional Categories

Abney's claim that only functional categories characteristically have overt subjects and that only functional categories contain AGR, lead him to posit that only the subject position of functional categories can be the landing site of movement by substitution. This claim seems to be valid for the functional categories of INFL and COMP in both languages. However, Spanish, unlike English, needs no movement analysis to account for genitive Case, as we will see in section 2.4.

Abney himself admits that it is difficult to classify certain categories with respect to their functional versus thematic features. He also states that the functional categories are asymmetric in their associations; INFL and COMP are both associated with verbal elements in language while determiners are related to nominal ones. These two points in isolation are not enough to cause a recategorization of determiners as lexical, however, they add support to my hypothesis that determiners in Spanish are lexical categories.

With respect to Abney's list of the differences between functional and lexical categories, many of the claims can be refuted. For example, (18a), the claim that functional categories are a closed class may be true but according to Emonds (1985), the only open categories which are possible in language are N, A, and V. That leaves various lexical and functional categories unable to accept new members.

I do not deny that there are differences between lexical and functional categories, however, the Spanish determiner seems to better suit the criteria which apply to lexical categories. For example, in the case of (18) c and d, we must admit that there are functional elements which are dependent, unstressed, or unable to be separated from their complements but there are also those determiners like demonstratives which do not fit this description at all. And (18e), the lack of descriptive ability, is relative to the category being analyzed. For Spanish determiners, I would argue that they have both the lexical form and meaning which characterizes a lexical category. Finally, in the case of (18f), Abney mentions some historical claims that there is a dichotomy in language between functional and lexical items. While he claims that this point is crucial, it does not provide a criterion for establishing whether a given category falls into one class or the other.

2.3.4. Differences between Spanish and English DPs

With regard to Abney's proposal for PRO in NP, this is another instance where the D as functional head in English solves problems previously unaccounted for in an NP analysis.

Additionally, Abney's analysis of AGR as the nominal equivalent of INFL may be supported very well by his comparison of modals in English to AGR since modals are often present and do show verbal inflection English but such is not the case in Spanish. Also assuming that Det and Infl have some sort of semantic connection is a little spurious in my opinion, since it was earlier claimed that functional categories have no semantic value.

A further problem for his analysis are the differences between Spanish and English DPs with regard to those determiners which head empty nominals in Spanish but are not allowed to do so in English. This difference which Abney does not discuss will be dealt with more extensively in Chapter Three.

According to Abney, it is generally thought that every word projects a phrasal node. He assumes that in the case of the determiner, XP, the determiner phrase, will provide both category X with lexical instantiations, and will provide determiners with specifiers (such as a possessor) and complements (a projection of N). In section 2.5, we will apply this configuration to Spanish in order to see if it fully accounts for Spanish determiner phrases.

Abney also states that two determiners in a row are ungrammatical which obviously in Romance, is not the case as seen in (39).

(39) a. mis tres libros 'my three books'
b. estos tres libros 'these three books'
c. mis otros tres libros 'my other three books'

The statement also needs modification for English since he classifies quantifiers and possessives as determiners and they can be found adjacent to each other: *my three books*.

2.3.5. Critique of Fukui and Speas

Fukui and Speas make claims similar to those of Abney, using Japanese and English as the representative languages for their proposal. We will deal with their analysis of the determiner as a functional category in this section. Their proposal does seem to work well for the languages they analyze, however, when applied to Spanish, some of their claims do not hold.

2.3.6. The Determiner as a Functional Category

Fukui and Speas claim that the determiner, like INFL and COMP, is a functional category with a unique specifier position that closes off its projection and does not allow iteration. They claim that because the determiner is a functional category and cannot iterate, we do not have sentences such as *the the man. The examples they use in (27) are also applicable to Spanish. The following sentences with more than one determiner are ungrammatical:

(40) a. *la la casa 'the the house'
b. *esta la casa 'this the house'
c. *mi la casa 'my the house'

A problem arises with regard to Spanish and (40c) because although that example is ungrammatical, *la mi casa* is acceptable in the Leonese dialect and Italian still uses the definite article together with the possessive adjective in the same type of construction. Other variations such as the emphatic form of the possessive adjective in Spanish *la casa mía* 'my house' or the use of the definite article with the demonstrative adjective as in *el hombre este* 'this man' are also problematic with regard to a unique specifier position for Functional categories and are perhaps better served by my determiner as lexical category hypothesis.

Another claim of Fukui and Speas is that functional categories cannot govern and Case mark into their complements since functional categories govern to the left. Functional categories also select a unique complement, according to Fukui and Speas. And finally, functional categories are said to be closed classes, lacking semantic qualities. I will admit that determiners are a closed class but as we saw in 2.3.3 so are other lexical and functional categories. While all of the other claims made about functional categories may be true in English and Japanese, they do not all hold true for Spanish. I will argue in 2.4 that Spanish determiners can govern and Case mark into their complements and also assign rightward Case, unlike a functional category. Furthermore, the movement analysis necessary for genitive Case assignment in English is neither necessary nor possible for Spanish.

2.4. PROPOSAL OF DETERMINER AS A LEXICAL CATEGORY IN SPANISH

In this section, it will be proposed that the determiner in Spanish is a lexical, not a functional category based on evidence counter to that presented by Abney and Fukui and Speas.

2.4.1. Motivation for the Proposal

A possible solution to the disparities between the Spanish and English determiner is my assumption that C and I are true functional categories while D is a functional category in English and a lexical category in Spanish.

My principal reason for this division is based on evidence that the richness of AGR in Spanish, unlike English, allows Spanish determiners to appear adjacent to empty NPs, governing and Case marking into their complements. This characteristic of Spanish determiners will be dealt with more fully in Chapter Three. Less important reasons are the functional category properties as outlined by Abney (section 2.1.5) and critiqued with regard to Spanish in section 2.1.4.

2.4.2. Iteration of Determiners in Spanish

In section 2.3, examples such as *la mi casa* were given to show that iteration of determiners is possible. This provides evidence for my hypothesis that the determiner in Spanish is a lexical category head similar to V and A and not a functional one as proposed by Abney and Fukui and Speas. In Spanish, the following phrases are also grammatical:

(41) a. los libros míos 'my books'
 b. estos libros míos 'these books of mine'
 c. estos tres libros míos 'these three books of mine'
 d. los libros estos 'these books'
 e. mis tres libros 'my three books'

Since we are not disputing Abney's hypothesis that the determiner is the head of its phrase, we will use a DP structure for the phrases in

(41). However, since I am claiming that the determiner in Spanish is a lexical category, I will follow Fukui and Speas' framework for lexical categories.

2.4.3. Structure of Determiner Phrases

In order to account for the phrases in (41), here is the structure I propose, using (41a) as an example:

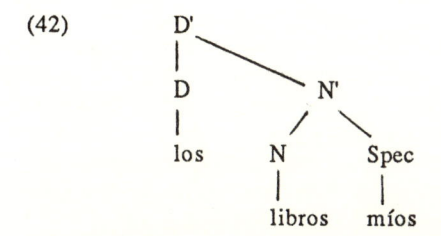

(42)
```
        D'
       / \
      D   N'
      |  / \
     los N  Spec
         |   |
       libros míos
```

Since Spec can be generated either to the right or left of N', in (42) it is rightward but in (43), on the left to account for (41e):

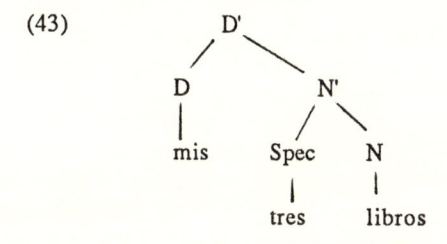

(43)
```
        D'
       / \
      D   N'
      |  / \
     mis Spec N
          |   |
         tres libros
```

In the case of (41c), the quantifier *tres* would be the head of its own phrase and *míos* is in a righthand Spec:

(44)
```
         D'
        /  \
       D    Q'
       |   /  \
     estos Q   N'
           |  /  \
          tres N   Spec
               |    |
             libros míos
```

For sentences such as *mis libros*, we will assume that the Spec of N' is where *mis* is generated. If *mis* moves to D to assign genitive case, the D must be empty to allow for this movement. This will also prevent *los mis libros*. However, in dialects such as Leonese (and languages like Italian), we want to be able to generate a definite article + possessive construction like *la mi casa* and this may be able to be handled like a clitic doubling construction. We will examine the possessive determiner phrase in more detail in Chapter Four.

2.5. CONCLUSIONS

In this chapter we have reviewed Abney's proposal that the determiner is the head of its own phrase and has a structure similar to that of the sentence. We have also discussed the arguments by Abney and Fukui and Speas that the determiner is a functional category. We have seen that for reasons of iteration and government that this categorization does not hold for the Spanish determiner. Reasons for Spanish determiners to be considered lexical and the structure for the lexical Spanish DP have also been given. We will now turn to a discussion of the Spanish definite article and demonstrative and their ability to govern empty categories.

NOTES TO CHAPTER 2

[1] However, ergative verbs such as *faltar* may have a postverbal subject which lacks an overt determiner as discussed in Contreras (1986).

[2] The exceptions include *that* which can co-occur with an AP: *that intelligent*. On the other hand, in English there are determiners such as *the* and *every* which are only found with NPs.

[3] Quoted in Makino (1968:12).
[4] Specifiers may iterate as long as they are fully licensed and interpretable at LF.
[5] Those languages such as Japanese which are said to lack functional categories also lack specifiers.

Chapter 3

Demonstratives and Definite Articles

3.0. INTRODUCTION

In this chapter, we will examine the definite article and the demonstrative in both Spanish and English. The basic properties of the two types of determiners will be discussed as well as the similarities and differences between the two. Of special concern is the empty nominal construction headed by either a definite article or demonstrative in Spanish. Two approaches to these structures, that of Torrego (1987) and Contreras (1989), will be studied and critiqued. Additionally, a proposal of Contreras (1986) concerning nouns which appear without a determiner in Spanish NPs will be examined. Finally, my own proposal that the determiner in Spanish is a lexical rather than a functional category will be applied to constructions involving definite articles and demonstratives.

3.1. THE DEFINITE ARTICLE

The definite article in both Spanish and English is responsible for more narrowly specifying one or more of a group of objects (Solé and Solé 1977). For example, the general statement *Vendo coches baratos.* 'I sell cheap cars.' can be further defined by the addition of the definite article: *Vendo los coches baratos.* 'I sell the cheap cars.' (as opposed to the expensive ones). The definite article in both languages can also be used with a singular noun to indicate an entire class of objects:

(1) La manzana es una fruta dulce.
'The apple is a sweet fruit.'
La hormiga es una criatura trabajadora.
'The ant is a hardworking creature.'

3.1.1. Omission of the Definite Article

On the other hand, the omission of the definite article in both Spanish and English occurs if an indefinite amount or portion of the noun is referred to:

(2) Hay coches en la calle. 'There are cars on the street.
Como manzanas. 'I eat apples.'
Escuchamos música de Brahms. 'We listen to Brahms' music.'

3.1.2. Gender and Number of the Definite Article

Another Spanish versus English article distinction, as is well known, is the gender / number manifestation. In Spanish, articles agree in gender and number with the nouns to which they refer. This gender assignment is arbitrary in relation to non-naturally occurring gender:

(3) a. el (masculine gender, singular number) vestido
(*o* indicates masculine gender, singular number) 'the dress'
b. la (feminine gender, singular number) corbata
(*a* indicates feminine gender, singular number) 'the necktie'

In addition to masculine and feminine gender assignment, Spanish has a neuter article *lo* which is used with an adjective but without a noun following it to express the idea of part, matter, or thing. English lacks this construction, instead using *the* + adjective + noun:

(4) Lo interesante de la música viene al final.
'The interesting part of the music comes at the end.'
Lo normal es que tenemos un examen los viernes.
'The normal thing is that we have a test on Fridays.'

3.1.3. Uses of the Definite Article

In spite of the similarities between the use of definite articles in Spanish and English, there are also many differences that surface. In Spanish, the definite article is used consistently to identify any unique object or concept; English may do this as well but the definite article is not obligatory and just as often the article is omitted and the noun is capitalized for identification as a proper noun:

(5) El mundo es redondo. 'The world is round.'
El infierno debe ser terrible. *'The hell must be terrible.'
*Infierno debe ser terrible. 'Hell must be terrible.'

The nouns in (5) are concerned with a unique thing or idea and as such are singular in number. However, with a plural noun denoting a generality or whole class, Spanish and English are opposites in their use of the definite article with a plural generic noun; English avoids its use:

(6) Los gatos son mis animales favoritos.
*'The cats are my favorite animal.'
*Gatos son mis animales favoritos.
'Cats are my favorite animal.'

3.1.4. Definite Article Without a Noun

Articles in Spanish can also be used in constructions which omit the noun. This ability to use the definite article without an overt noun to form a nominal clause is a phenomenon that Spanish has which is not available in English:

(7) Me trajo los que quería.
*'To me he brought the (masculine plural) that I wanted.'
'He brought me the ones that I wanted.'

In (7), *los*, together with the restrictive clause *que quería* 'that I wanted' forms a nominal clause.

3.2. TORREGO'S ANALYSIS OF EMPTY NOUN PHRASES

Torrego (1987) argues that the empty noun in such nominals is pro and cites evidence from not only Spanish but also Italian, Catalan, and Portuguese.[1] Torrego notes that the '*el* nominal construction', her term for the determiner phrase lacking an overt noun, does have restrictions with regard to the type of complement it allows that a regular NP does not exhibit.

3.2.1. Restrictions on *el* Nominals

A primary restriction is that of only allowing a prepositional phrase complement that is headed by *de* 'of'. Those prepositions other than *de* which head a complement to an *el* nominal result in ungrammaticality as seen in Torrego's examples:[2]

(8) a. El [e] de las Meninas no está en este museo.
   'The (one) of the Meninas is not in this museum.'
   b. Presenciaron los *(asaltos) a las zonas urbanas.
   'They witnessed the (assaults) to the urban areas.'
   c. Les aburren las *(conversaciones) sobre animales.
   'They get bored with the (conversations) about animals.'

However, if the prepositional phrase headed by a preposition other than *de* is preceded by a *de* phrase, the phrase containing an *el* nominal is grammatical:

(9) a. *el por Melibea
   b. el de Pleberio por Melibea
   'the (one) (= love) of Pleberio towards Melibea'
   (Torrego 1987, 95)

Unlike PP complements, there seem to be no restrictions on adjectives appearing adjacent to an empty noun phrase and the adjective can intervene between the empty noun and a PP other than the one headed by *de* :[3]

(10) a. Las [e] fáciles están en la mesa.
   'The easy (ones) are on the table.'
   b. *Leyeron las por Unamuno.
   'They read the (ones) by Unamuno.'

c. Leyeron las buenas por Unamuno.
   'They read the good (ones) by Unamuno.'

Another possible complement to an *el* nominal is a relative clause but only one headed by the complementizer *que* 'that':

(11) a. Hablé con [el [e]] [que estabas].
     'I talked to the (one) you were with.'
   b. *Hablé con [el [e]] [con quien estabas].
     'I spoke to the (one) with whom you were.'

A further restriction on the definite article is that it cannot appear alone, unlike an empty nominal headed by a demonstrative:

(12) a. Me acompañó al [e] *(del banco).
   b. Me acompañó a ese (del banco).
     'She accompanied me to *the / that (one) of the bank.'

3.2.2. The *el* Nominal versus the *este* Nominal

Torrego says that the fact that the Spanish definite article is often claimed to be a clitic (because of its ability to combine with one syllable prepositions) is not a sufficient explanation for the difference in status between nominals headed by a demonstrative and those headed by a definite article. She calls the demonstrative a stronger determiner than an article in Spanish because a nominal headed by a demonstrative as in (12b) can occur syntactically in the same positions as a noun phrase with an overt head. The distribution of *el* nominals is the same but there are restrictions which characterize the *el* nominal as we saw in section 3.2.1. The examples in (13) illustrate an *este* versus an *el* nominal:

(13) a. También acaban de salir estos sobre anatomía.
     'There also just appear these about anatomy.'
   b. También acaban de salir *los sobre anatomía.
     'There also just appear the (ones) about anatomy.'

The lack of restrictions on an *este* nominal and its ability to occur without modification causes Torrego to assume that the definite article but not the demonstrative is able to 'lend itself to variation' (p. 99), a notion that she does not define further.

3.2.3. Categorizing the Empty Element in a Nominal

Because of the lack of restriction on the positioning of both *este* and *el* nominals, Torrego assumes that their empty elements are not subject to the Empty Category Principal (ECP). The ECP as formulated by Chomsky (1981) requires that every empty category be properly governed. Instead of requiring the empty element to be properly governed, Torrego assumes the empty category in *este* and *el* nominals to be either pro or PRO. She claims that demonstratives are content words with different variations (the three in Spanish being *este* 'this', *ese* ' that', and *aquel* 'that') and as such, are heads which have the correct person, gender, and number features to license pro. The definite article, however, as a 'weaker' determiner may or may not be able to license pro through its features.

3.2.4. 'Strong' versus 'Weak' Determiners

Weakness in determiners seems to be a relative term because immediately after claiming that Spanish definite articles are weak in relation to demonstratives, Torrego claims that they are stronger than the definite article in French and Italian. This lack of strength in the latter two languages is supported by data such as the following Italian examples from Torrego:

(14) a. Il [e] rosso 'The red (one)'
b. *Il [e] di Durer / Quello [e] di Durer
'The (one) of Durer / That (one) of Durer'
c. *Il [e] che ti ho detto / Quello [e] che ti ho detto.
'The (one) that I have given to you /That (one) that I have given to you'

The *el* nominal construction in Italian can only occur if there is some kind of adjective to modify it as in (14a), not with a PP or clause, as in the ungrammatical (14b), (14c). These latter constructions require the empty noun to be preceded by a demonstrative. This leads Torrego to suggest that perhaps demonstratives and the Spanish definite article have the gender and number features seen when an overt noun is present in the NP. She proposes that words with semantic content are able to have their own inflectional features. It does not matter where the agreement process takes place, between D and NP, (a feature of D as Torrego claims) or as an AGR phrase that comes between D and NP.

In any case, the Romance demonstrative and the Spanish definite article are strong enough to support the necessary AGR features.

On the other hand, 'weak' determiners such as the Italian and French definite article (and the so-called 'weak' form of the Spanish definite article) are unable to have strong AGR features.[4] A factor that Torrego considers important in this ability or lack thereof to support AGR features is the lack of person features in the definite article. According to Borer (1986), person, number, and gender are the features necessary to license pro. To make up for this deficiency of the Spanish definite article, Torrego posits that the definite article can license pro as long as something else, such as a modifier that is [+N] which will carry person, features, gives D its necessary person features.[5]

3.2.5. PPs with *el* Nominals

Those elliptical NPs headed by a definite article according to Torrego are restricted in the type of modification they allow due to the way in which they are able to license pro. As we have seen earlier, PPs which have actual semantic content are not allowed in *el* nominal phrases unless an adjective, a relative clause headed by *que*, or PP headed by *de* is positioned between the preposition and the empty NP. Torrego states that the difference between a true prepositional phrase and those limited modifiers allowed with *el* nominals is that the latter group of modifiers is [+N] while a true prepositional phrase is [-N] since prepositions are characterized as [-N, -V]. She suggests that the restricted status of true PPs indicates that the *de* type of PP found with *el* nominals is most likely a nominal modifier with the *de* inserted as a default preposition. *De* is not considered to have the semantic value of what Torrego calls 'true prepositions', i.e., those like *sobre*.

In the same vein, the relative clause with a PP in the {SPEC, CP] is limited enough that *que* introduced relative clauses allowed with an *el* nominal have an empty operator in the specifier of CP. Torrego claims that in Romance, this must be an NP (or DP) as shown in her example (15) which follows.

(15) Calisto consiguió el amor de Melibea por el que tanto había luchado.
'Calisto got the love of Melibea for which he had fought so much.'

Consequently, since C as the head of its phrase agrees with its Spec, a *que* introduced relative clause is [+N] at S-structure.

Those modifiers which are [+N] contain person features and are said to be the source of person features absent from the gender / number AGR features found in the definite article. Torrego assumes that these AGR features are in [SPEC, DP] position. A PP whose head is a preposition with semantic content is [-N] and will not be able to pass person features to D in order to license pro, as in (13b). Of course, if there is a [+N] modifier which comes between the [-N] element and the empty noun nominal, pro is licensed and the structure is grammatical as in (10c). Torrego does not offer any structural representations of the claims proposed here.

3.2.6. Empty Nominal Structure

According to the assumptions about empty categories proposed in Chomsky (1981), the empty category in a nominal phrase could be either PRO, pro, an anaphor, or a variable. Torrego eliminates the latter two categories without discussion. Also PRO, because of its inability to be in a governed position, would not be the choice for this position, since it appears as though it is governed by the definite article as seen in the structural representation below.

(16) [$_{DP}$ [D' los] [$_{NP}$ e]]

The elliptical category in these elliptical nominal phrases must then be pro. It is common to assume that part of pro's licensing conditions lie in its ability to be governed. Torrego points out that under an NP-analysis, *el* does not govern pro because *el* will be the head of a DP found in the specifier position of NP:

(17) a. [$_{NP}$ [Spec el [$_{N}$]]]
     b. [$_{NP}$ [$_{DP}$ el] [$_{N'}$ pro ...]]

Because DP is a maximal projection, it is a barrier to government under the assumptions outlined in Chapter One. Even if pro were considered as N or N', there would be no way for the head of DP to govern pro.[6] In order to achieve the structure where D will serve as pro's governor, D needs to be a sister to pro:

(18) [$_{DP}$ [$_{D'}$ el] [$_{NP}$ pro]]

Unless this empty category is assumed to be pro and is able to be licensed through government, no other empty category can be thought of as being able to fill the position in the empty nominal due to the considerations previously defined in Chapter One such as government (in the case of PRO) and binding (of anaphors and variables) that rule them out.[7]

3.2.7. The Referent of pro in *el* Nominals

Another consideration in the matter of pro in *el* nominals is the reference pro can have with regard to an antecedent. Until now, we have assumed that pro could refer to any antecedent previously mentioned in the discourse so that the gender and number of the *el* nominal which follows is evident. In (19), the antecedent of the *el* nominal is the masculine singular noun *café* ' coffee':

(19) A: ¿Vas a comprar café? 'Are you going to buy coffee?'
B: Sí, voy a comprar el de Colombia. 'Yes, I'm going to buy the (one) from Colombia.'

However, unlike ordinary pro, the pro in *el* nominals is said by Torrego to require c-command by its antecedent:

(20) a. [La gente que colecciona los [e]$_i$ / *$_j$ de arte] siempre compra los libros$_j$ de esta editorial.
'The people that collect the (ones) about Art always buy the books of this Publishing Company.'
b. Los amigos de Juan$_i$ se parecen a los [e]$_i$ de Pedro.
'The friends of Juan's look like the (ones) of Pedro's.'
c. *Los de [e]$_i$ Juan se parecen a los amigos$_i$ de Pedro.
'The (ones) of Juan's look like the friends of Pedro's.'
(Torrego, 105)

In (20a), [e] cannot refer to *libros* and in (20c), [e] cannot be interpreted as 'friends'. Only in (20b), where the empty category element pro is c-commanded by its antecedent *amigos*, can the two co-refer. But if the [e] and *friends* cannot be interpreted as coreferential in (20c), this cannot be due to Principle C of the binding theory, because Principle B of the binding theory would then rule out the acceptability of (20b).[8]

However, pro's bound pronoun status has an additional restriction in *el* nominals: pro cannot be overtly realized in an elliptical nominal, as shown in the ungrammatical (21b):

(21) a. las que viven en Seattle 'the (ones) that live in Seattle'
b. *las ellas que viven en Seattle 'the they that live in Seattle'

Torrego rejects Montalbetti's (1985) claim that bound interpretation of pronouns in Spanish can only occur if the pronoun is not overtly present in the sentence. For example, the sentence *Muchos cantantes creen que son fantásticos.* 'Many singers think they are fantastic.' can only have coreference between 'many singers' and 'they' in Spanish if *ellos* 'they' is left unexpressed. But Montalbetti also noticed that in certain syntactic structures, Spanish overt pronouns can also be bound: *Muchos cantantes creen que la gente dice que ellos son fantásticos.* 'Many singers think that people say that they are fantastic.', in which *ellos* is bound by *muchos cantantes*. Since the pro of an elliptical nominal can never be expressed by a pronoun, it is possible that pro in these constructions is not the same kind of pronoun as can be given overt form. Torrego offers no solution except to suggest that the pro in *el* nominals is perhaps an NP instead of a DP.

3.3. CRITIQUE OF TORREGO'S ANALYSIS

In this section, we will review Torrego's claim that the empty category in *el* and *este* nominals is pro. I will also discuss my own arguments in favor of the determiner as a lexical category in light of Torrego's work.

I agree with Torrego that the difference in status between *el* and *este* nominals, the former being subject to restrictions not applicable to *este* nominals, does not seem to be due to a clitic-like status of the definite article in Spanish. The evidence for a definite article stronger than a clitic is the Spanish definite article's ability to appear without an overt noun in a phrase such as (21a).

However, unlike Torrego, I would argue that the demonstrative, is identical to the definite article with respect to person features. Both have masculine and feminine forms and singular and plural ones, and as far as overt person features, the two elements appear to be identical. The demonstrative has either the same lack of person features as the definite article or both the definite article and the demonstrative bear third person features, an assumption that seems intuitively correct given the ability of an NP headed by a demonstrative to occur in the same contexts as regular NPs. The distribution of the *este* nominal is relevant because it bears none of the restrictions which apply to the *el* nominal with respect to the environment in which it occurs. Although the *el* nominal has restrictions which the *este* nominal does not have, the notion of a 'weak' definite article determiner in Spanish which is somehow 'stronger' than its Italian or French counterpart does not seem to be more explanatory than simply stating that there are certain differences between *este* and *el* nominals in Spanish.

Torrego's proposal that words with semantic content are able to have their own inflectional features and that Spanish demonstratives and determiners are strong enough to support AGR features is consistent with my hypothesis that the determiner is a lexical category. By stating that these determiners have semantic content, my notion of lexicality is supported because it is lexical, not functional categories which are said to have semantic content if we use Abney's guidelines.

I also disagree with Torrego's characterization of *de* as not a true preposition. This notion is suspect since *de* seems able to assign Case and appear in all contexts where true prepositions occur. However, this is a minor point.

My biggest disagreement with Torrego is her choice of pro as the empty category present in elliptical nominal constructions. I think the Contreras proposal which will be discussed in 3.5 is a more explanatory approach to dealing with the empty nominal construction in Spanish. His proposal is consistent with the ECP definition which I stated in Chapter One.

3.4. BOSQUE'S ANALYSIS OF EMPTY NOMINALS

Arguing that some specifiers can be proper governors, Bosque (1986) offers evidence which accounts for the ability of some NP specifiers to be proper governors in Spanish yet not in English. He reasons that examples such as (22) are grammatical in Spanish but not in English due to the Spanish definite article's gender and number properties that English articles do not have.

(22) Conozco al padre de Pepe y al [$_N$ e] de Jorge.
    *'I know the father of Pepe and the [$_N$ e] of Jorge.'

Thus, in Spanish there is agreement between the head noun and its specifier- a type of feature sharing, which allows the specifier to be a proper governor for an empty N or N'.[9] This Spec-Head agreement as proposed in Chomsky (1986a) can be seen in the structure of (23):

(23)
```
      N'
     / \
    N   XP
       /  \
      XP   X'
      |   / \
      X⁰ ZP
          |
          Z⁰
```

On the other hand, the specifiers of VP, AP, and PP do not exhibit Spec-Head agreement and because of that, cannot properly govern an empty category. Bosque assumes the notion of Spec-Head agreement from Chomsky (1986a), paraphrased in (24), to account for examples like (22):

(24) An external governor governs specifier x iff the head of x is governed.

According to Bosque, the possessive, which can be seen in the following example, unlike the definite article and demonstrative in Spanish, only agrees in number; it is not strong enough to have the Spec-Head agreement which would qualify it as a proper governor:

(25) *Traiga Ud. sus libros y mis [$_N$ e] 'Bring your books and my [$_N$ e].'

An obvious problem with that argument are the Spanish possessives *nuestro/a/os/as* 'our' (first person plural) and *vuestro/a/os/as* 'your' (familiar, second person plural). These possessives have gender, number, and person; therefore they should be able to serve as proper governors for empty nominals but cannot. Furthermore, in languages such as French which have gender/number agreement of possessives with their heads, the head of the phrase cannot be empty:[10]

(26) *ton voyage et mon [$_N$ e] 'your trip and my [$_N$ e]'

The problems and possible solutions with regard to the possessive will be dealt with more extensively in Chapter Four.

Another problem that Bosque's analysis does not solve can be in example (27): a numeral can serve as a proper governor of an empty N in both Spanish and English without any obvious Spec-Head agreement and furthermore, an English genitive can do the same as seen in (28):

(27) Cociné dos platos de pescado y tres de [$_N$ e] pollo.
'I cooked two plates of fish and three [$_N$ e] of chicken.
(28) I finished Mary's [$_{N'}$ e] because she had eaten too much.

With so many counterexamples to the hypothesis of specifier as proper governor, we need to find an approach which better accounts for the data already seen.

3.5. CONTRERAS' ANALYSIS OF EMPTY NOMINALS

The empty nominal phrase is the focus of a work by Contreras (1989) who begins his discourse by rejecting the proposals made by Bosque (1986) and Lobeck (1986) that specifiers can be proper governors. Although he acknowledges that this notion could account for the fact that the Spanish definite article can precede an empty N and the English article cannot if the two languages were characterized as having different parameters, the idea of specifier as proper governor actually creates more problems than it solves.

3.5.1. Problems with the Specifier-as-Proper-Governor Analysis

First, in a sentence such as (29), one would have to admit maximal projections as well as lexical items in specifier position as proper governors.

(29) Since Bill's [$_{N'}$ e] is being fixed, we'll take Mary's car. (Contreras 1989:84)

Then both X^{max} and X^0 would be allowed to be empty as well as any intervening projections, which Contreras considers unmotivated.

Additionally, if the specifier of N can govern an empty N', we should then assume that the same would be true for the specifier of IP's ability to govern an empty INFL. (According to Chomsky (1986), the specifier of IP is the subject). The subject cannot govern an empty I' as seen in Contreras's example:

(30) *Since Bill [$_{I'}$ e], I think Bill's mother also loves Mary.

A further implication of the specifier as proper governor hypothesis is an ad hoc restriction on which categories can or cannot serve as proper governor. In English and Spanish, neither the specifier of AP, VP, or PP can be a proper governor, as shown in the following examples:

(31) a. *Ella es bien guapa y él es muy [$_{A'}$ e].
'She is very pretty and he is very [$_{A'}$ e].'
b. *Muchas veces iba a la playa y ella siempre [$_{V'}$ e].
'Many times I went to the beach and she always [$_{V'}$ e].'
c. *Los papeles están debajo de la mesa y los libros están casi [$_{P'}$ e].
'The papers are under the table and the books are [$_{P'}$ e].'
d. El hombre que conocemos y el [$_{N'}$ e] que no conocemos.
'The man that we know and the [$_{N'}$ e] that we don't know.'
e. *Nuestro coche verde y su [$_{N'}$ e] rojo.
'Our green car and their [$_{N'}$ e] red.'

All of the sentences in (31) have elements in their Specs which should be able to serve as a proper governor of the empty category if we were to assume that the Specifiers can properly govern. However, we note that only example (31d) is grammatical. This evidence, in addition to the other previously mentioned problems causes Contreras to reject this approach to proper government.

3.5.2. Empirical Data Contra Bosque

Contreras concludes that the lack of empirically motivated assumptions by Bosque and Lobeck with regard to specifier as proper governor requires the consideration of another approach in order to account for sentences such as those in (32).[11]

(32) a. Vi al estudiante de física y al [$_N$ e] de química.
'I saw the student of physics and the [student] of chemistry.'
b. María compró tres libros de física y Juan compró dos [$_{N'}$ e].
'Mary bought three books on physics and John bought two.'
c. Dame este libro de física y ese de [$_N$ e] química.
'Give me this book on physics and that [book] on chemistry.'

d. Como el [$_{N'}$ e] de María está en reparaciones, usaremos el auto de Juan.
'Since Mary's is being repaired, we'll use John's car.'
e. *Su libro sobre Borges es mejor que su [$_{N'}$ e] sobre Cortázar.
'His book on Borges is better than his/her [book] on Cortázar.'

These sentences provide evidence that an empty N or N' can appear following a definite article, a numeral, or a demonstrative in Spanish but not following a possessive adjective in the determiner position. A discussion of the latter construction will be dealt with in Chapter Four but an examination of the other empty nominals in light of Contreras' work follows.

3.5.3. Theoretical Considerations

Contreras begins by suggesting that the empty categories in nominals such as (32) are nonmaximal ones, N and N'. Unlike Torrego, however, Contreras argues that the empty element in phrases such as those in (32) must obey the ECP, using a version of Stowell's (1985) Head Government Requirement (HGR):

(33) [e] must be governed by an X^0 category.

A problem arises with the use of the HGR as a requirement for empty categories. Since N and N' as nonmaximal will not be subject to the HGR, a solution must be offered to account for the grammaticality (or lack thereof) of the examples in (32).

(34) HGR (Revised): [e] must be head governed by a proper governor.

3.5.4. Binding Theory Considerations

An additional consideration with regard to the type of nominals in sentences such as (32 a-d) is the fact that empty categories are limited as to type and their adherence to one of the 3 principles of the Binding theory as submitted by Chomsky (1982). Thus, it is necessary to categorize N and N' based on these considerations. Contreras concludes that they are [-pronominal, -anaphor] and therefore fall under Principle C of the Binding theory which states that such an NP must be free in the domain of its A' binder (Chomsky 1986). Since no operator binds the empty categories under consideration, this contradicts the notion that the features [-pronominal, -anaphor] are equivalent to the term *variable*.[12]

3.5.5. The Determiner as a Functional Head

Contreras adopts Fukui and Speas's previously discussed theory of determiners as functional heads in order to account for sentences such as those in (32). According to their hypothesis, X^0s are the only categories which can serve as proper governors but this status extends to both lexical and functional categories.

3.5.6. Theoretical Considerations

To summarize the categories as given in Chapter Two, the lexical categories according to Fukui and Speas are N, V, A, and P. The functional categories proposed are INFL, COMP, and DET. In addition to the Case assigning abilities of lexical categories V and P, certain functional elements are able to assign case, so Fukui and Speas combine lexical and functional case assigning abilities under the term Kase. Those functional elements able to assign Kase through their Functional Features (F-Features) are nominative Case assigned by INFL's tense/agreement component, genitive Case said to be assigned by *'s*, and +WH assigned by a WH-COMP. The non-Kase assigning items are *to* in an IP, *the* in a DP, and *that* in a CP. In addition to the Kase proposal, the structure of DP according to Fukui and Speas is the following:

(35) [$_{DP}$ [$_{D'}$ DET N']]

Since all lexical categories project to X', N' is considered a maximal projection so intermediate ECs are unnecessary and the only categories which are allowed to be empty are X^{max} and X^0. Functional categories like DET on the other hand are subject to the Functional Projection Theorem:

(36) A Functional head projects to X" iff Kase is to be discharged to its spec position. Otherwise, it projects only to X'.

3.5.7. Advantages to the Determiner-as-Functional-Head

A clear advantage to the Fukui and Speas approach is that proper government of empty categories can be accomplished through head government since a functional head such as a determiner is the head of its phrase. Nevertheless, not all the standard lexical categories are considered proper governors; V, A, and N are but P is not.[13] Among the functional categories, not even all the functional heads of the same category can be considered proper governors.

Another benefit of the Fukui and Speas proposal is that it solves the problem we saw in sentences like (31). Due to the fact that items like *muy* and *siempre* are not the heads of their phrases, they cannot govern an EC, as illustrated by the ungrammaticality of (31) a and b. And (30), repeated here as (37) is ungrammatical because a subject is not a functional or lexical head, causing the ECP to be violated.

(37) *Since Bill [$_{I'}$ e], I think Bill's mother also loves Mary.

In contrast, (29) repeated here as (38), is fine because within the Fukui and Speas approach, the functional head 's is a proper governor, not the X^{max} to its left.

(38) Since Bill's [$_{N'}$ e] is being fixed, we'll take Mary's car.

3.5.8. A Parallel Situation: The Quantifier as Head of Phrase

Contreras finds the determiner situation with regard to proper government parallel to that of some quantifiers which occur with an empty nominal. Certain quantifiers are proper governors and others are not. In (39), the quantifiers can properly govern but the examples in (40) cannot:

(39) a. Aunque algunas tiendas ofrecen este servicio, muchas [$_{N'}$ e] no lo ofrecen.
'Although some stores offer this service, many [$_{N'}$ e] don't offer it.'
b. Con respecto a sus hijos, varios [$_{N'}$ e] viven en Seattle.
'With regard to his children, several [$_{N'}$ e] live in Seattle.'

(40) a. *Aunque todo coche tiene sus problemas, no todo [_N'_ e] funciona mal.
*'Although every car has its problems, not every [_N'_ e] works badly.'
b. *Todas las mujeres viven aquí pero cada [_N'_ e] vive en su propia casa.'
'All the women live here but each lives in her own home.'

Contreras suggests that the reason for grammaticality differences between the two groups above is a matter of structural difference. He proposes (41a) as the structure for the examples in (39) and (41b) for those in (40):

(41) a. [_QP_ Q XP]
b. [_N'_ Spec [N']]

In (41a), it is easy to see that Q is the head of its phrase and consequently, it can properly govern the empty N's of sentences like (39). On the other hand, the quantifiers of (41b) are located in the specifier position of N' and as such cannot serve as proper governors. Since Contreras previously rejected the Specifier as proper governor proposals of Lobeck and Bosque due to inadequate empirical evidence, a quantifier in a specifier position will not be able to govern properly.

Independent support for the separate structures in (41) comes from the ability of those considered quantifier heads as in (41a), to occur in conjunction with a DP or to be the head of a partitive expression while those considered to be specifiers do not have these properties:

(42) a. toda la gente 'all the people'
b. todas las casas 'all the houses'
c. *cada la gente *'every the people'
d. *cada las casas *'every the houses'

(43) a. muchas de las casas 'many of the houses'
b. varias de las casas 'several of the houses'
c. *cada de las casas *'every of the houses'

Assuming the structures in (41) also accounts for the grammaticality of (44) in contrast to (40a):

(44) Puedo ayudarte con algunos problemas pero no todos [e].
'I can help you with some problems but not all.'

In (44), *todo* is the head of category Q and can govern the empty DP which is its sister. On the other hand, *todo* in (40a) is in the Spec of N' and as it is not the head of the phrase cannot properly govern the EC.

Within the Fukui and Speas framework, phrases such as *muchos problemas* 'many problems' can also be accounted for. We have already seen that *muchos* can co-occur with an empty category so Contreras predicts that it is a functional head even though it appears as though its sister *problemas* is not a maximal projection. But since we have previously noted that N' in this system is X^{max}, Contreras suggests that the actual structure of *muchos problemas* could be [$_{QP}$ [$_Q$ muchos [$_{N'}$ problemas]]].

3.6. DISCUSSION OF CONTRERAS (1989)

In this section, we will review Contreras' proposal and show that it is the best way in which to account for the Spanish empty nominal structure. Of course, I claim the determiner as lexical category in Spanish but that does not affect any of Contreras' claims made in 3.5.

After finding so many counterexamples to Bosque and Lobeck's proposals of specifier as proper governor, Contreras applies Fukui and Speas' proposal that the determiner is the head of its own phrase and accounts for examples such as those in (32).[14] However, my hypothesis of DET as a lexical head of its phrase still conforms to the Head Government Requirement and also accounts for examples like (32).

The only example left unaccounted for in (32) was that of the possessor which headed the empty nominal phrase in (32e) but we will discuss that construction in Chapter Four.

The X^0 determiners analyzed in section 3.5.2 were able to serve as proper governors of the empty categories they headed. I propose that the determiner is lexical but under the Fukui and Speas proposal adopted by Contreras, lexical X^0s are able to govern also. In this way, examples (32a-d) are still properly governed. His proposal also seems valid for quantifiers which is of added explanatory benefit to linguistic theory. However, my proposal would also account for quantifiers, although they are not at issue in this work.

A proposal of Contreras' that I will adopt is that the empty category in elliptical nominals is a [-anaphor] [-pronominal] as defined by Koopman and Sportiche (1982). As I have stated before, the ECP definition I adopt requires proper government of all empty categories and Contreras' proposal fits in well with that definition.

3.7. DEFINITE ARTICLE IN SUBJECT POSITION

As we have seen in previous examples, a noun preceded by a definite article can serve various syntactic functions in a sentence- the object of a preposition, direct object, and subject- but the similarities between definite article usage in Spanish and English vary in regard to the subject position. A noun used without a definite article in subject position is quite common in English but a bare noun in the same position in Spanish is much more restricted.

3.7.1. Contreras' (1986) Analysis of Bare NPs

Contreras (1986) analyzes Spanish bare subject NP sentences in terms of the ECP. In sentences such as *Quiero café*. 'I want coffee', *Falta café* 'Coffee is needed', and **Me gusta café* 'I like coffee', the noun phrase containing *café* is said to have the structure [$_{NP}$ [$_{QP}$ e] N'] and the empty QP in these sentences needs to be properly governed. Contreras adopts Kayne's (1981a, b) government hypothesis which allows lexical categories to govern across one maximal projection, but no more than one. With respect to the verbs in the sentence above, *faltar* 'to lack' and *quedar* 'to remain' are classified as ergative verbs (those verbs whose subject is in object position while *gustar* 'to like' and *acabarse* 'to finish' are not. Since ergative verbs like *faltar* do not have their subject move to the postverbal position, the empty QP can be properly governed by the verb, as seen in (45).

(45) INFL [$_{VP}$ [$_{V'}$ falta [$_{NP}$ [$_{QP}$ e] café]^i] [$_{NP}$ pro]^i]

3.7.2. Spanish as a VOS Language

A further assumption Contreras makes is that Spanish is a VOS language, not SVO as commonly thought. If Spanish were to be classified as SVO, then the sentence **Me gusta café* should be grammatical but it is not. This grammaticality would occur as a result of the empty QP's government by the INFL of the verb *gusta* as seen in (46):

(46) [$_S$ [$_{VP}$ [V' me gusta INFL [$_{NP}$ [$_{QP}$ e café] N']]]]

3.7.3. Accounting for SVO Word Order

Contreras must also account for those sentences in Spanish whose word order is SVO since sentences such as (47) are common in Spanish:

(47) [$_S$ [$_{NP}$ las chicas]$_i$ [$_S$ INFL [$_{VP}$ [$_{V'}$ caminan]t$_i$]]] 'The girls walk.'

Contreras calls these SVO sentences pseudo-topic constructions and posits that their preverbal NPs are adjoined to S (IP) via movement, unlike true topics which are generated in situ. These adjoined NPs are subject to the ECP and therefore cannot occur with an empty determiner:

(48) *[$_S$ [$_{NP}$ e chicas]$_i$ [$_S$ INFL [$_{VP}$ [$_{V'}$ caminan]t$_i$]]]

Since e is ungoverned in sentences such as (48), the result is ungrammatical.

3.7.4. Accounting for Plural NPs without Determiners

How do we account for sentences like (49) which is fine and (50) which is not:

(49) Viejos y niños escuchaban con atención sus palabras.
'Old people and children listened attentively to his/her words.'
(from Bello 1847)

(50) *Café y leche son caros.
'Coffee and milk are expensive.'

According to Contreras, a plural bare NP can be in the subject position of a nonergative verb if it is linked to another plural bare NP by a conjunction. But this does not hold true for singular NPs. There must be something that conjoined plural NPs have in common which can override the ECP but Contreras does not have an answer for this or for the type of sentence which has a nonergative verb with an NP in focused position.

3.7.5. Plural Bare Nouns in Topic Position

Again, in these sentences, the plural bare noun creates a grammatical sentence but the singular does not:

(51) a. La cosecha la destruyeron LANGOSTAS.
'The crop was destroyed by GRASSHOPPERS.'
(from Suñer 1982a, 213)
b. LANGOSTAS destruyeron las cosechas.
'GRASSHOPPERS destroyed the crop.'
c. *Esas manchas las produce CAFE.
'Those stains are caused by COFFEE.'
d. *CAFE produce esas manchas.
'COFFEE causes those stains.'
(from Contreras 1986, 46)

The focused bare noun construction is not grammatical with all plural nouns, so a generalization which extends to this type of sentence as applicable to plural vs. singular focused NPs is not possible. Although the ECP would seem to disallow all such constructions, obviously some other much more specific properties are involved in focused structures than in non-focused NP clauses.

3.7.6. Empty QPs with Mass Nouns

In spite of unanswered questions about focused constructions, Contreras also deals with non-focused NP structures in his work and uses as support for his empty QP hypothesis the fact that unlike English, the bare NP in Spanish has a partitive, not a generic interpretation:

(52) Quiero café. = Quiero algo de café. 'I want some coffee.'
Quiero tortillas. = Quiero algunas tortillas. 'I want some tortillas.'
*Café es caro. 'Coffee is expensive.'

The other support he has for his analysis of empty QPs applies only to mass nouns like *café* when used with certain transitive verbs such as *terminar* 'to finish'. If a mass noun is used with a quantified direct object and a verb like *terminar*, the resulting sentence is ungrammatical, as is the same sentence with a bare direct object:

(53) *Terminé mucho café. 'I finished much coffee.'
*Terminé café. 'I finished coffee.'
Terminé el café. 'I finished the coffee.'

3.7.7. Evidence for a Parallelism Condition

If a bare NP is in a preverbal focused or topic context the sentence is grammatical, as these subjects may be bare and are not subject to the ECP:

(54) Café no creo que tengan. (Café is the topic)
 'Coffee I don't think they have.'
 Esclavos construyeron las pirámides. (Esclavos is the focused subject)
 'Slaves built the pyramids.'

However, not all bare NPs are able to be located in the topic position. This must be accounted for since the structure of the ungrammatical sentence in (55a) appears to be exactly like its grammatical counterpart (55b). Contreras gives the following examples:

(55) a. *Café no creo que sea caro.
  'Coffee I don't think it's expensive.'
 b. Café no creo que haya.
  'Coffee I don't think there is (any).'

The difference in grammaticality between (55) a and b is that in b, the topic is coindexed with a bare NP which is in a position where its empty QP is governed but the same is not true for a. Contreras first proposes the structures in (56) to account for the sentences in (55). However, simply coindexing the topic with an NP variable is not enough to distinguish (56) a from b:

(56) a. *[$_{NP}$ e café]$_i$ [$_{S'}$ no creo que [INFL sea caro e$_i$]]
 b. [$_{NP}$ e café]$_i$ [$_{S'}$ no creo que [INFL haya e$_i$]]

In (56a), INFL governs e$_i$ and in (56b) the verb *haya* governs e$_i$. Since both empty positions are governed, the sentences should both be fine but (56a) of course, is not. Contreras proposes a parallelism condition which requires the topic to have the same internal structure as its coindexed variable. More formally:

(57) Parallelism Condition: In the structure X...Y where X is a topic, and Y is its coindexed variable, X and Y must have the same categorial structure.

The parallelism condition divides e_i into an empty Q and an empty N' so that the structure of the grammatical topic sentence in (56b) is now (58):

(58) [$_{NP}$ [$_{QP}$ e] café]$_i$ ...[$_{NP}$ [$_{QP}$ e] e]$_i$

With a structure such as (58), only the [$_{QP}$ e] on the far right is properly governed as in (56b), the sentence with a parallel topic/coindexed variable.

3.7.8. Proper Government of Spanish Bare NPs

Unlike topic constructions, those NPs which serve as the subject of a nonergative verb must have either a determiner or if the determiner (QP in Contreras' work) is empty, the empty QP must be properly governed by X (X is either a V or P):

(59) [$_{X'}$ X [$_{NP}$ [$_{QP}$ e] N']]

The definition of government which best captures the grammaticality or lack thereof in the Spanish bare NP examples seen earlier is Kayne's (1981a) proposal that a lexical category can govern across one but not more than one S (IP) type boundary. In addition, Kayne suggests that government across one NP boundary is also possible. By adopting this theory of government, Contreras can account for the data presented previously in this section by assuming the structure below, where X^0 can govern across NP into the empty QP:

(60) X^0 [$_{NP}$ [$_{QP}$ e] N']

The formal definition of K(ayne) government is as follows:

(61) A lexical category governs its sisters and the categories immediately dominated by its sisters.

But due to governing properties yet to be satisfactorily explained, Contreras finds it necessary to exclude N as a proper governor, although he calls the measure an ad hoc one. The only two lexical categories which qualify as governors according to Contreras are V and P.[15]

3.8. DISCUSSION OF CONTRERAS (1986)

In this section, we will discuss the Contreras work which deals with bare nouns in subject position in Spanish.

Due to a need for government of empty categories, Contreras takes an ECP approach to account for the ungrammaticality of bare nouns in subject position in Spanish. Since he proposes a VOS word order for Spanish, he can account for the sentences such as *Falta café* ' and for the ungrammaticality of **Me gusta café* but he fails to account for the conjoined plural constructions like the sentence in (49), repeated here as (62):

(62) Viejos y niños escuchaban con atención sus palabras.

Also a focused bare NP such as (51b), repeated here as (63) is grammatical but not all focused plural bare NPs are grammatical:

(63) Langostas destruyeron las cosechas.

The ECP analysis simply is not enough to account for all of the discrepancies with respect to topic and focused constructions; as Contreras notes, there must be more specific properties involved in these structures in Spanish.

Another point which I would have liked to seen extended to more verbs than just *terminar* involved *terminar*'s use with a mass noun and a quantified direct object. A sentence such as **Terminé mucho café* is as ungrammatical as the corresponding bare noun construction. But *terminar* was the only verb given as an example and the restrictions such as the application to certain transitive verbs, quantified direct objects, and mass nouns is limited in its ability to account for other sentences with empty QPs.

My biggest question in regard to an ECP approach to bare nouns is not addressed by Contreras because it concerns English. Why are bare nouns in subject position allowed in English but not in Spanish? The answers to this and the other questions left answered by this work are all topics worthy of future linguistic investigation.

3.9. CONCLUSIONS

In this chapter we have reviewed work by Torrego and Contreras concerning empty nominals in Spanish. The Contreras approach which involves compliance with the ECP has been shown to provide the best explanation of the empirical evidence. We have also looked at bare nouns without determiners and the resulting ungrammaticality when they occur in subject position in Spanish. The Contreras proposal applying the ECP to this phenomenon leaves unanswered questions about bare nouns in certain types of constructions.

We have also seen in this chapter that although both Spanish and English definite articles are the heads of DP, *el* can properly govern and *the* cannot. This could be due to the 'richness' of the Spanish article which is inflected for gender and number as opposed to the English article which is not. However, we have also noted that the possessive determiner *mi* cannot properly govern an empty category. Reasons and possible solutions to this problem will be examined in more detail in Chapter Four.

NOTES TO CHAPTER 3

[1] For simplicity's sake, the following discussion will use Spanish examples but they will be applicable to the previously mentioned languages.

[2] Torrego mentions that Spanish does have true propositions possible after empty nominal phrases: *la sin huesos* 'the one without bones' (= the tongue) but these are said to be adjectival and not very productive.

[3] Torrego notes that there are adjectives which cannot occur in this kind of construction but a discussion of them would take her work too far afield.

[4] It is interesting to note that non-pro drop languages such as French do not have strong enough AGR features to license pro even though in the case of French possessive determiners the elements of person, number, and gender are present:

*Ma voiture et ta [e] 'My car and yours'

[5] Borer claims that in Hebrew the unmarked third person is unable to license pro. Torrego counters that in Spanish, third person features, even those given by default in the case of adjectives, are enough to license pro but perhaps the referential versus nonreferential quality of pro is the key to the differences in grammaticality in the two languages.

[6] Torrego's definition of government is based on Chomsky (1986b).

[7]Torrego says that *el* in isolation cannot be thought of as a DP in these constructions but she does not discuss this point any further.

[8]Haik (1984) noted that bound pronouns have to be c-commanded by their antecedents at S-structure and Torrego suggests that because of this restriction of c-command that pro must be treated like a bound variable in Spanish *el* nominals. However, Torrego gives a counterexample to the c-command restriction from Uriagereka (p.c.):

(i) Juan conoció todas las salas del museo a partir del día en que su madre le llevó a conocer la de Goya. 'Juan knew of all the rooms of the Museum from the day in which his mother brought him to know the (one) of Goya.'

Torrego comments that this sentence merely demonstrates that an *el* nominal's antecedent can appear in an empty Topic position as part of an adverbial clause (a partir del día en que...).

[9]Spec-Head agreement according to Chomsky (1986) provides for an external governor to govern a specifier x if and only if the head of x is governed.

[10]Contreras has mentioned that perhaps French possessives and articles are clitics which cannot bridge an empty category. He notes that the Spanish definite articles may have the same status, since a totally null N' which co-occurs with an article is ungrammatical (example i). However, the article can cliticize across an empty category if there is something overt in N' (example ii):

(i) *No me senté porque el [$_N$ e] tenía tanta gente. 'I didn't sit down because the [$_N$ e] had so many people.'
(ii) Mientras el hijo de Pepe miraba la televisión, el [$_{N'}$ e] de Carlos leía.
'While Pepe's son watched television, the [$_{N'}$ e] of Carlos read.'

[11]Contreras briefly mentions a notion explored by Napoli (1985) that empty categories do not exist and that the specifier in constructions like (20) is nominal. A major drawback to this proposal is that the Spanish definite article and the English genitive are thus viewed as pronouns since they are found in Spec.

[12]This also supports the Koopman and Sportiche (1982) idea of a variable as defined by its context, not merely an empty category subdivision.

[13]The problem of P as proper governor remains controversial. Kayne (1981) claims that P does not properly govern, while Huang (1982) says that it does.

[14]Since Contreras provides extensive arguments against the Spec as proper governor hypothesis, I will not analyze the Bosque proposal separately.

[15]My own proposal that the determiner is a lexical category rather than a functional one and is capable of proper government is supported by Contreras (1989) although his proposal is somewhat different.

Chapter 4

The Possessive and Genitive

4.0. INTRODUCTION

The possessive determiner in Spanish is more difficult to categorize with regard to its ability or lack thereof to govern an empty category than the definite article or demonstrative. It is, however, much easier to account for the Spanish genitive than for its English counterpart. The *'s* which assigns genitive Case in English is an anomalous element that is not found in the majority of the world's languages. Therefore its ability to be a case assigner is of interest since the proposals for the English genitive may or may not be applicable to other languages. In this chapter we will consider various proposals dealing with the assignment of genitive Case in both English and Spanish. We will first discuss proposals made by Chomsky (1986b), Abney (1987), and Fukui and Speas (1986) with regard to the English genitive. We will also examine the work of Mallén (1988) who specifically treats the topic of Spanish possessives. In addition, Contreras' (1989) discussion of the inability of the Spanish possessive to properly govern an empty category will be studied. Finally, we will attempt to account for the possessive determiner as a lexical category comparable to the way in which we dealt with the definite article and demonstrative in Chapter Three.

4.1. THE GENITIVE ANALYSIS OF CHOMSKY (1986b)

In this section, we will examine the proposal of Chomsky (1986b) for the assignment of genitive Case in English. Structurally, it is harder to account for the genitive in English than in Spanish. Chomsky attempts to explain English genitive Case assignment by stating that the lexical head of a nominal phrase, unlike the V, directly θ-marks both its specifier and complement positions inherently at D-structure. One must account for the fact that English has two kinds of genitives, those preceded by *of* and those followed by *'s*.

(1) a. [$_{NP}$ the [$_{N'}$ [$_{NOUN}$ growth] [$_{NP}$ the child]]]
    b. [$_{NP}$ the child's [$_{N'}$ [$_{NOUN}$ growth] t]]]

In such structures, the NOUN θ-marks and gives Case to its complement at D-structure. At S-structure, the NOUN governs its complement and the Spec of NP so Case can be realized in either of the two positions by affixing some element, *of* in the complement position or a possessive element in [Spec, NP] which would account for the dual possibility of genitive Case assignment in English. However, there are problems that result from the movement of NOUN's complement in (1b) since it received its Case at D-structure. Unless the genitive Case moves with the noun it was assigned to, the condition on chains that they have only one Case marked position will be violated because both the original site of the noun and the landing site for the movement are Case marked positions. The current assumption is that θ-roles are assigned from one specified position to another so that the position which is assigned a θ-role originally would be the recipient of the genitive Case.

4.2. ABNEY'S ANALYSIS OF THE ENGLISH GENITIVE

In this section, we will discuss Abney's proposal regarding the assignment of genitive Case in English.

Within Abney's DP analysis, it is necessary to account for the way in which the possessor is assigned Case. Abney observes that it is normally assumed that *'s* assigns Case. However, the genitive assignment in English does not follow genitive assignment in other world languages. As far as the position of *'s* and its relationship to the possessor, Abney rejects the notion of *'s* as simply a morphological affix, saying that since it can be cliticized to the whole subject NP, it is not merely an affix on the head of an NP:

(2) [the whole world]'s problem
    [the woman in the park]'s picnic basket

Neither does *'s* seem to be a prenominal Case assigner nor does the proposal that N assigns genitive Case to the possessor seem to work. To accomplish the latter, Abney says that N would have to license the possessive determiner presumably through q assignment which he rejects. Abney instead analyzes *'s* as a postposition instance of AGR, which marks the genitive Case. Since the Det is always empty when there is a possessor (in English), he suggests a solution of determiner elision as a possibility. Determiner elision would entail that originally there was a determiner with definite interpretation in the position that the possessor may also occupy. If a possessor is inserted into this position, the determiner is deleted but the definiteness is somehow retained. This turns the problem of non-co-occurrence of a determiner and possessor into an advantage because it can explain why if the determiner and possessor occupy the same position there is no determiner ever present in possessive constructions yet possessives retain a definite interpretation. For instance, in English the NP in (3a) is grammatical but (3b) is not.

(3) a. *a hundred nights*
    b. **hundred nights*
    c. **those [a hundred] nights*
    d. *those [øhundred] nights*

In the same way (3c) is ungrammatical but (3d) is fine. Abney claims that *a* is required before *hundred* unless a determiner goes before *hundred* causing *a* to be deleted. The structure for a phrase such as (3d) can be found below:

(4)
```
            DP
           /  \
         Spec  D'
          |   /  \
        those D   NP
              |   |
           hundred N'
                   |
                   N
                   |
                 nights
```

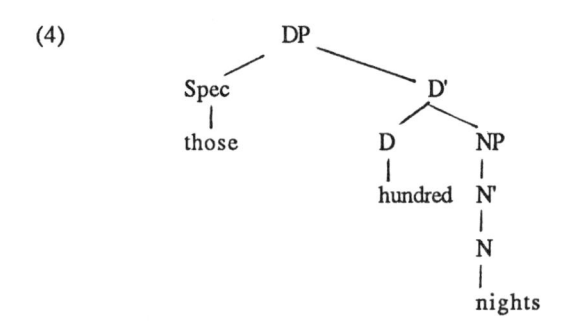

Even if the possessor/determiner conflict is resolved in this way, it is still necessary to decide if the genitive *'s* is present at D-structure or is inserted at S-structure. To avoid problems with passivization of noun phrases, Abney suggests that *'s* be viewed as a Case marker which is a functional element that inherits the referential index and descriptive component of its complement. A noun raises to the Spec of D in order to receive the genitive Case given by AGR. Thus, Abney proposes that *'s* is present at D-structure and is a Case marker rather than a determiner for the historical reason that *'s* has traditionally been seen as a morpheme marking the genitive case. Assuming *'s* to be a Case marker also accounts for languages like Hungarian where possessors and lexical determiners are found together; he claims that *'s* as Case marker generalizes to languages like this whereas *'s* as determiner does not.

4.3. ANALYSIS OF ABNEY WITH RESPECT TO SPANISH

In this section, we will review Abney's approach to the genitive in light of evidence from Spanish and the problems which arise.

His analysis of the genitive is not readily applicable to Spanish; there is no *'s* to assign genitive Case and no need to posit a movement of the Noun to the Spec of D in order to receive that Case. In English, the functional determiner *'s* assigns genitive Case; in Spanish, since Case assignment is always to the right, we can posit the rightward assignment of genitive Case as well.

Another phenomenon in English that is not applicable to Spanish is the complementary distribution of a determiner such as *the* and the genitive *'s*. In Spanish, a definite article is a necessary part of the so-called long form of the possessive and can also be found together with a *de* phrase to show ownership:

(5) a. el libro suyo 'his book'
    b. el libro de Juan 'John's book'

Abney also encounters a problem with the elision analysis that he proposes with respect to relative clauses introduced by the determiner *the* which cannot be introduced by a possessor. For example:

(6) a. *the violin that I played*
    b. **Julia's violin that I played*

If there is a determiner deleted in (6b) and the sentence is actually *Julia's the violin that I played* before that deletion at PF, it would seem that his proposal is specifically targeted to English. As we have noted before, the *'s* is not the norm for genitive Case in the majority of the world's languages. In fact, the Spanish version of (6b), seen in (7), is grammatical:

(7) el violín de Julia que (yo) toqué 'Julia's violin that I played'

Abney mentions an alternative to the deletion analysis for determiners which is more desirable because it does not use *'s* as the basis for the notion. The concept that there is a type of co-occurrence restriction that restrains nominal AGR from appearing in a D node if a lexical determiner is present is specifically applicable to English but is not based on the *'s* itself. In English, a lexical determiner such as *the* has no AGR features and as such will be in complementary distribution with AGR whose instantiation is *'s*. This alternative prevents a possessor from appearing when a determiner such as a definite article is already present in a phrase because the possessor would have no way to receive Case, as we saw in the ungrammatical (6b).

The Abney proposal of the determiner elision of *a* is also not necessary for Spanish as the numerical determiners such as *hundred* do not co-occur with this determiner:

(8) a. *cien noches* 'a hundred nights'
    b. *esas cien noches* 'those hundred nights'
    c. *sus cien noches* 'his/her hundred nights'

He goes on to say that two determiners in a row are ungrammatical which the following Spanish examples will show is not true, although the determiners are of different types:

(9) a. mis tres libros 'my three books'

b. la mi libro 'my book' (Leonese dialect)
c. los tres libros suyos 'his/her three books'

In conclusion, we note that while Abney's explanation of genitive Case in English is sufficient, it fails to account for Spanish genitives and possessives.

4.4. FUKUI'S TREATMENT OF GENITIVE CASE IN ENGLISH

In this section, we will review the proposal that Fukui makes for the English genitive. Fukui (1986) proposes that while the IN-argument of a VP can receive its case from the lexical head, the EX-argument generated inside a VP must move up to a Spec position where it receives its Case from INFL. A similar situation occurs in noun phrases; an EX-argument generated inside NP must raise in order to receive genitive Case from a functional node which parallels INFL at the sentential level. This movement depicting the assignment of genitive Case is shown in (10):

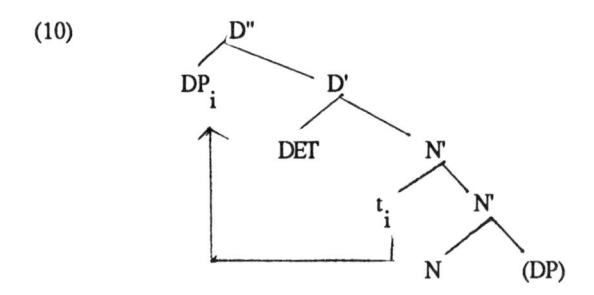

(10)

```
              D"
            /    \
         DP_i     D'
                /    \
             DET      N'
                     /  \
                  t_i    N'
                        /  \
                       N   (DP)
```

4.5. DISCUSSION OF FUKUI AND SPEAS' PROPOSAL FOR GENITIVE CASE: SPANISH VERSUS ENGLISH

In this section we will discuss the differences between assignment of genitive Case in Spanish and English, using Fukui and Speas' (1986) proposal for English as a basis for the discussion.

In English, according to Fukui and Speas, the appearance of a functional determiner head is in complementary distribution with the genitive *'s* case marker. The following examples will illustrate this point[1]:

(11) a. *John('s) the/that/some book

However, in Spanish, a Det head can be found with a *de* plus possessor phrase which indicates genitive case as seen in the following sentences.

(12) a. el libro de Juan 'John's book'
b. este libro de Juan 'this book of John's'
c. algún libro de Juan 'some book of John's'

Fukui and Speas claim that in English the *'s* assigns Kase whereas *a*, *the*, and other determiners do not. This lack of Kase assigning f-features for determiners other than *'s* explains why the sentences in (13) are ungrammatical:

(13) a. *I enjoyed Mary *the* book
b. *I enjoyed Mary *a* book

For Spanish, we can assume that *de* assigns Kase as a lexical item since prepositions perform this role elsewhere in the grammar as seen in (14a) where *de* assigns Kase to its object *casa*. In (14b), *de* assigns Kase to *Juan*:

(14) a. Vendió muchas cosas de la casa.
'He sold many things from the house.'
b. Vendió muchas cosas de Juan.
'He sold many of John's things.'

Support for the assumption that genitive case is assigned by an F-feature in English and by a lexical category in Spanish derives from the consideration, mentioned in Chapter Two, that functional heads such as determiners assign Kase to the left, unlike lexical categories which assign rightward Kase. For the *'s* to assign Kase by virtue of its F-feature, a noun in English must raise to the D position as seen in (15).

(15) a. John's hat
b.
```
            D"
           /  \
         DP_i   D'
          |    /  \
        John  Det  N'
              |   /  \
             's  t_i  N'
                      |
                      N
                      |
                      hat
```

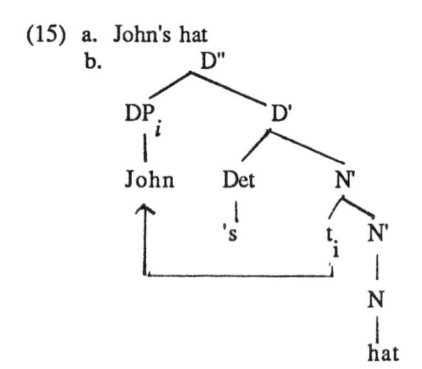

However, since genitive Case assignment in Spanish is not accomplished by means of *'s*, a different structure will have to be proposed and we will see that structure illustrated in section 4.10.

According to Chomsky, as we saw in section 4.1, there is a second environment in which a noun phrase can receive genitive case in English: by means of an inserted preposition. As explained in Chapter One, Section 1.1.4, all noun phrases must receive Case. If a noun phrase does not receive Case, the resulting sentence is ungrammatical which is why the sentence with two adjacent noun phrases in (16) is unacceptable:

(16) *I saw the destruction the city

However, since prepositions can assign Case, the preposition *of* can be inserted before the second NP in (16) to create a grammatical sentence:

(17) I saw the destruction of the city.

In the same way, genitive Case in English can either be assigned by the *'s* or by the insertion of the preposition *of*. Two examples, (18a) to illustrate the *'s* assignment of the genitive and (18b) to show genitive Case by an inserted preposition are given below:

(18) a. the city's destruction
b. the destruction of the city

It is also possible to have a more complex construction where there are two arguments:

(19) a. the Roman's destruction of the city
    b. the city's destruction by the Romans

Since nouns are not able to assign structural case, either argument, *Roman* or *city*, may raise to D and the argument not raised to D will receive Case from a preposition inserted after the movement. The movement and preposition insertion for (19) a and b are illustrated in (20) a and b respectively:

(20) a. [$_{DP}$ the Roman$_i$ [$_{D'}$'s [$_{N'}$ t$_i$ destruction of the city]]]
    b. [$_{DP}$ the city$_i$ [$_{D'}$'s [$_{N'}$ destruction t$_i$ by the Romans]]]

Fukui and Speas expand this concept by claiming that any NP (DP) can raise to receive the Kase assigned by D even if that DP is not an argument of N. They give as examples the sentences in (21):

(21) a. The city's destruction by the Romans
    b. The Roman's destruction of the city
    c. Yesterday's destruction of the city by the Romans

However, this ability of any DP to raise to D produces the following question: How does one prevent inserted prepositions, even if they are limited to *of* and *by*, from generating phrases such as *the Roman's destruction by the city* or *the city's destruction of the Romans*. In other words, are there restrictions on the thematic role borne by NPs which co-occur with particular Case assigners? Also when Fukui and Speas state that any NP may move to the Spec of DP, do they have in mind a restricted group such as *yesterday* which they call NP adverbs or is any NP available for this movement? The answers to these questions may lie in θ-theory considerations or in selectional restrictions inherent in nouns like *destruction*, as we will see in Section 4.6.7.

4.6. MALLEN'S PROPOSAL FOR POSSESSIVE PHRASES

The discussion in this section will be centered around Mallén's (1988) arguments for an intermediate nominal projection NINFL and his characterization of that element versus a parallel functional category QUAN. He uses Spanish as the primary language to illustrate his ideas and deals extensively with movement out of Spanish DPs. We will only consider his movement analysis in a limited way since movement out of Spanish possessives is, according to Mallén, impossible.

4.6.1. The Structure of QP

In order to fit quantifiers and possessives into the same structural configuration as NPs, Mallén proposes that there is an intermediate nominal projection NINFL which can optionally be filled by a quantifier. The QP whose head is QUAN is allowed to assign genitive Case either leftward or to the right depending on the language in question. In English, QUAN assigns genitive Case to its left, requiring that an external argument inside the lexical maximal projection raise to [Spec, DP] in order to meet the Visibility Condition (see Chapter One, Section 1.1.4). In contrast to English, languages such as Spanish are said to have a QUAN which gives rightward Case assignment which allows the external argument to stay inside the NP. Since the [Spec, DP] in Spanish is then left unfilled, Mallén suggests that it can then be filled by a non-argument such as a Possessor. He argues that in this way, there is no difference between the structure of a sentence and an NP. He claims that in both cases two functional heads, (CP/IP, DP/QP) dominate a lexical projection (VP, NP) and because of the structural similarities, the same effects of barriers to government which apply to sentences will apply to NPs. The structure he proposes for NINFL (nominal INFL) and its maximal projection NIP can be seen in (22):

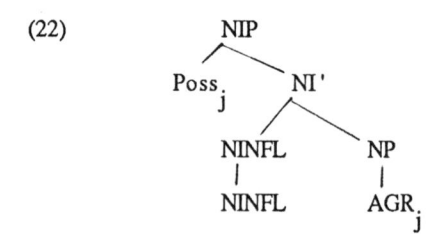

(22)   NIP
              /   \
         Poss$_j$ NI'
                   / \
               NINFL   NP
                 | |
               NINFL   AGR$_j$

The determiner is the lexical realization of the functional category NINFL. Mallén adopts Fukui's (1986) categorization of the determiner as functional, for reasons of iteration, uniqueness of complement selection and prenominal positioning. Since F-heads of the same type cannot iterate and always precede the rest of the NP in head first languages like English and Spanish, Mallén claims that this provides evidence for the D as head of its own category. But unlike COMP and INFL, D can select not only for NP as a complement but also VP, CP, and DP. Mallén gives the following example of a D selecting for a complement DP:

(23) [$_{DP}$ [$_{D'}$ [$_D$ aquellos [$_{DP}$ de los hombres]]]] 'those of the men'

The partitive *of* phrase behaves exactly like any other nominal complement but we need to assume that D is the head of its phrase and not the specifier of an NP since only heads can select for complements.

4.6.2. Possessives and Ex- versus In-arguments

Mallén explains that, in accordance with the Lexicalist Hypothesis of Chomsky (1970), current theory supports the notion that instead of deriving nouns from their verbal equivalents, a verb and its related nominal counterpart will have the same thematic (θ) grids. This is important with respect to possessives because it helps to explain why the type of NPs that can be found in the possessive position in deverbal nominals corresponds to the group of possible EX-arguments in the related verbs.

Both nouns and verbs have an external (EX) argument and an internal (IN) one with which they relate according to their θ specifications. The ability of a nominal projection to have the same structure as is found at the sentence level is a desirable generalization because it may better account for the rapidity of language acquisition. In languages like French, Italian, and Spanish, the EX-argument is more structurally prominent than the IN-argument, according to Mallén. This gives the EX-argument certain authority that the IN-argument lacks. For example, only pronominal arguments can be found in the specifier which precedes NP. If an element is to be raised out of NP to the Spec position, the EX-argument has priority over the IN-argument and neither argument can raise if there is a possessive which dominates them. In fact, it will be the possessive itself that is in the Spec of NP. Thus, extraction of an IN-argument over an EX-argument or a possessive is forbidden as is the movement of an EX-argument over a possessor. Mallén gives the following examples:

(24) a. su retrato de Gertrude Stein
'his (agnt) portrait of Gertrude Stein (objt)'
b. *el de Gertrude Stein retrato
*'the of Gertrude Stein portrait'
c. *su (objt) retrato de Picasso (agnt)
*'his (objt) portrait by Picasso'

d. *su (agnt) retrato de ese coleccionista (poss)
   *'his (agnt) portrait of that collector'
e. su (poss) retrato de Gertrude Stein (objt) de Picasso (agnt)
   'his (poss) portrait of Gertrude Stein by Picasso'

The key factor in all of the above sentences is the hierarchy of possessor over both agent and object and agent over object when extraction is involved. Possessors therefore are not affected by the existence of either the EX- or IN-argument in a phrase since they c-command both of them within NP.[2]

4.6.3. Genitive Case and θ role for Spanish NPs

As we saw in section 4.2, Abney proposes that genitive Case is assigned when an NP raises to receive the Case given by the functional element similar to INFL. Mallén suggests, contra Abney, that genitive Case can be assigned by the noun or by QUAN in conjunction with what he calls the null preposition *de*. The figure he offers in (25) is similar to the assignment of nominative Case in a sentence but he gives no empirical evidence to support his structure and aid the reader:

(25) [$_{DP}$Spec[$_{D'}$[$_{QP}$Spec[$_{Q'}$QUAN[$_{NP}$ex-arg[$_{N'}$NOUNin-arg]]]]]]

with Genitive arrows from D' to Spec of QP, and from N' to ex-arg; Move α from Spec of QP.

Mallén categorizes the determiners, quantifiers, and nouns in Spanish as weak Case assigners. Due to that weakness, they need the assistance of the preposition *de* which is inserted to support the Case assigning head. Genitive Case in Spanish is thus said to be assigned by the head and *de* working together as co-assigners of Case.

Since Case is assigned under government, Mallén states that possessors, EX-, and IN-arguments are assigned their Case in situ by determiner, quantifier, and noun respectively. He claims that just because the EX-argument does not have to raise to [Spec, QP] in Spanish does not explain why the EX-argument should not occur to the left of the noun in Spanish. In English, the specifier must be on the left side of the head for purposes of Case because QUAN and/or DET assign Case through Spec-Head agreement to the left. But in Spanish, all full NP arguments specified in the lexical frame of a nominal head will appear after that head:

(26)
```
         DP
        /  \
     Spec   D'
           /  \
         DET   QP
              /  \
             Q'   Spec
            /  \    \
         QUAN   NP   de-phrase(Poss)
         /  \   |
      QUAN  AGR N'
              /  \
          NOUN   IN-arg   EX-arg
                  |         |
               de-phrase  de-phrase
```

He assumes as does Rivero (1986) that the postposition of Spanish NPs is due to directionality of Case and θ role assignment which is always to the right in Spanish.

4.6.4. Pronominal Possessives

Modifiers such as possessives also appear to the right of the head they modify but this cannot be motivated by directionality according to Mallén. He accounts for the position of possessives by assuming that they do not receive any θ-role but that they, like other modifiers in Spanish, always adjoin to the right of the head in unmarked cases.

However, the form of the possessive that Mallén calls pronominal can occur before the noun in Spanish:

(27) su$_i$ caricatura del político$_j$
   'his (agnt) caricature of-the politician (objt)'

To account for this fact, Mallén adopts the proposal of Rivero (1986) that possessive pronominals in Spanish are actually nominal clitics. The cliticization process incorporates the possessive clitic to the F-head QUAN, leaving behind a trace in its D-structure position. To illustrate this, Mallén posits the construction below with arrows showing the incorporation movement at S-structure:

(28)
```
              QP
              |
              Q'
            /    \
         QUAN     NP
        /   \    /  \
     suᵢ   QUAN N'   tᵢ
                / \
             NOUN  DPⱼ
```

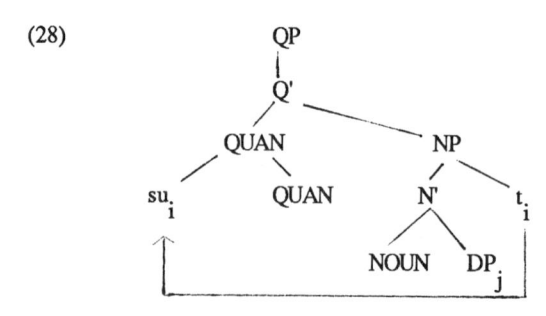

Because of the trace's need for proper government, no barrier should come between *su* and the trace in the NP. In (28), Q' is a potential barrier but it is not crossed and thus Mallén's structure proves suitable for the generation of prenominal *su*. In fact, the trace left by *su* also has the same effect on extraction out of the phrase as a lexical item would. Because of this, after the possessive cliticizes to QUAN, the trace prevents wh-movement of any IN-argument[3]:

(29) *ese es el político del queᵢ he visto susⱼ (varias) caricaturas
'that is the politician of whom (objt) I-have seen his (agnt) (several) caricatures'

As was mentioned earlier in this section, QUAN in association with *de* is said by Mallén to assign genitive Case to the EX-argument found in [Spec, NP]. However, once a possessive cliticizes to QUAN, QUAN can only assign Case to an element coindexed with the clitic itself. This is applicable in instances of Clitic-doubling where QUAN + *de* assign Case and θ-role to both the clitic and the doubled element through coindexing. Mallén says that this explains why a lexically realized EX-argument such as (30) is not possible if QUAN has an element other than the EX-argument itself cliticized to it:

(30) a. [$_{QP}$ [$_{Q'}$ [$_Q$ QUAN suⱼ] [$_{NP}$ [$_{N'}$ foto] de él] tⱼ]]
'his picture of him'
b. *[$_{QP}$ [$_{Q'}$ [$_Q$ QUAN suⱼ] [$_{NP}$ [$_{N'}$ foto tⱼ] de Juanⱼ]]]
'his picture of Juan'

Mallén does admit that the possibility of cliticization for the possessive does not exist in English because in English the possessive must move to [Spec, QP] to get Case from QUAN. However, if there is an EX-argument inside NP, the movement will be blocked because the Q' between the possessive and its trace will be a barrier to the trace's government:

(31) *[$_{NIP}$ its$_j$ [$_{NI'}$ NI [$_{NP}$ PRO [$_{N'}$ explanation t$_j$]]]]

4.6.5. The Character of QUAN

With regard to the possessive, we must discuss the QUAN (NINFL) category proposed by Mallén as its characterization relates to the way in which the possessive differs from other determiners. The label quantifier for Mallén includes not only quantifiers but also cardinal numbers, semi-numerals, and group nouns. Group nouns include those like *bunch* and *share* and Mallén gives the following sentences to show the licensing relationship between *Fred*, the subject of the predicate and *share*, the group noun in QUAN:

(32) a. Fred's share of blame for the accident.
b. *Fred's blame for the accident.

Unlike *share*, *blame* cannot license *Fred's* in (32b) because there is no element in QUAN to license the appearance of a possessive. Mallén claims that it is a filled QUAN and not a possessive morpheme which gives this licensing since *blame* as a lexical head cannot license the possessive.

It is difficult to decide if the group nouns should be included under the QUAN heading but Mallén claims that the entire spectrum which he has designated as QUAN are F-heads which select for a unique complement. QUAN is said to be selected by DET in unmarked cases and QUAN (= NINFL), whose projections are Q' and QP, selects for NP. The agreement (AGR) for QUAN is adjoined to it at D-structure. The structural configuration for Mallén's proposal can be seen in (33):

(33)
```
            DP
           /  \
        Spec   D'
              /  \
            DET   QP
                 /  \
              Poss   Q'
                    /  \
                 QUAN   NP
                 /  \   / \
             QUAN AGR ex-arg N'
                      |      |
                     NOUN   in-arg
```

4.6.6. Advantages of Mallén's Proposal

Mallén's analysis uses the structure in (33) to account for some difficulties with possessors that previously had less than satisfactory explanations. For example, the difference between 'alienable' and inalienable possessors can be structurally mapped onto (33) with the result that their restrictions are accounted for. 'Alienable' possessors are those which are not given a θ-role by the lexical head and using (33) as a model, would be found in [Spec, QP]. Since inalienable possessors are those which are so closely related to the noun that they are given a θ- role, they would be generated in [Spec, NP], an option that structure (33) makes available.

Another difficulty concerning possessors that the structure depicted in (33) attempts to account for is the ability of a Spanish phrase to contain both a possessor and an agent while in English, Mallén claims that possessors and agents are mutually exclusive:

(34) a. Vendió unos libros de Vargas Llosa (agnt) de estos estudiantes (poss). 'He sold some books by Vargas Llosa of these students.'
b. *He sold these students' books of Vargas Llosa's.

Mallén thinks that a distinction between possessives and agentive possessives is necessary due to languages like Spanish and Italian whose phrases can include both and this analysis provides for that relationship.[4] He argues that the hierarchically higher possessive has a rather loose relation to the lexical head while the lower element, the agentive possessive, has its interpretation limited by the θ-role given to it by a nominal projection. By proposing that the possessive is generated in the Spec of QP while the agent is found in the Spec of NP, structure (33) can account for the appearance of both items in the same construction. Additionally, the possessive will have scope over the agent because the QP where it is located is higher than the NP.[5]

Another possessor/agent dilemma that arises in generating these elements inside NP is that of both item's ability to fill the role of 'subject', depending upon the sentence. Possessors, as noted before, are higher in position in the NP than agents and as such have scope over them. Arguments such as objects or agents cannot be Wh- moved when a possessive is present higher in the phrase and it does not matter if the NP is preceded by a determiner/demonstrative or a quantifier/group noun, no extraction can take place. Mallén notes that when a possessor is realized in [Spec, QP], the QUAN projects to QP and extraction of the EX-argument of the NOUN would have to cross both NP and QP. The EX-argument would then land in [Spec, DP] after leaving an ungoverned trace in [Spec, NP] as shown in Mallén's depiction of that movement:

(35)

```
          V'
         / \
        V   DP
           /  \
         t_j   D' (= M barrier)
              /  \
          (DET)   QP = Barrier
            |    /  \
           DP  QUAN   Q'
                     / \
                    N'  NP
                   / \   |
                NOUN DP  t_j
```

Because of the inability to extract out of possessives, Mallén's proposed structure (33) also accounts for his examples below where the possessive in (36a) cannot be generated inside the complement and then through movement achieve its S-structure position.

(36) a. John's praise of strict parents
b. Fred's bunch of cows
c. ??? I have never understood Chomsky's bunch of proposals
d. they brought Peter's bunch of books from home

In (36a), *John* is not interpreted as having strict parents but in (36b) which seems to have the same S-structure, *Fred* is the possessor of the *cows*. Mallén explains this in relation to the possessor generated in the Spec of QUAN which allows a possessor relationship between *Fred* and the F-head *bunch* which can choose a DP or NP complement. He claims that in phrases like (36b) the possessor cannot have been raised from out of the *of* complement but his evidence lies in the peculiarity of (36c) when compared to (36b). He argues that *Chomsky* in (36c) should be interpreted as the agent, not the possessor and as such, the agent would be generated inside the complement NP and then moved to the Spec of the functional head, something which Mallén deems impossible. In any case, Mallén claims that in (36b, d) the grammaticality stems from the possessive's ability to be generated in situ in [Spec, QP]. Since *praise* in (36a) is not a group noun, its lack of QUAN cannot license the possessive relationship between *John's* and *parents*. But Mallén subsequently needs to explain how *John's* and *praise* acquire their possessive relationship and why (36a) is grammatical which he does not do.

4.6.7. R-nominals versus P-nominals

Mallén offers a distinction between the kinds of nouns that QUAN F-selects for to help explain the difference in their ability to co-occur with a possessive. Those nouns which depict the result of a process (R-nominals) have a possessive variable which obtains a value from an element in [Spec, QP] (said to be the possessor) via Modification as proposed by Zubizarreta (1987). Just like other modifiers, the possessor is only optional in the specifier position and QUAN will project to either Q' or QP depending on the filling or lack thereof in the Spec. Mallén offers the following structure to illustrate his proposal for R-nominals:

(37)   QP
                                |
        Poss -modification ⟶ Q'   x
                             QUAN   NP

In contrast to R-nominals, nominals which denote a process or event (P-nominals) are claimed by Mallén to be unable to have a possessive variable. This is said to be due to the nature of the P-nominal itself since it describes an event or process rather than something quantifiable. He claims that an element occupying the [Spec, QP] position of a P-nominal cannot be interpreted as a possessive because there is no ability to assign a value to a variable. The QUAN of a P-nominal is said to lack [± count] features, is unable to be filled with a Quantifier, Group noun, semi-numeral, Cardinal number, or plurality features and is able to be modified by *no* which other QUANs cannot. The examples in (38) are Mallén's examples of P-nominals

(38) a. *Mañana anunciaremos tu distribución.
         poss
    'Tomorrow we will announce your distribution.'
  b. La no cancelación del concierto tuvo funestas consecuencias.
    'The non-cancellation of the concert had terrible consequences.'

He explains that Zubizarreta (1987) divides P-nominals into two classes: A and B. The class A nominals are derived from verbs like *traducir* 'to translate' and *describir* 'to describe'. These nominals can appear with either the preposition *de* or *por* which translates as 'by'. On the other hand, the class B nominals, derived from verbs like *destruir* 'to destroy' and *asesinar* 'to assassinate' can only appear with *por*, not *de*:

(39) a. la descripción del paisaje de/por Pedro
    'the description of the landscape by Pedro'
  b. la destrucción de la ciudad *de/por los soldados
    'the destruction of the city by the soldiers'

Another difference between class A and B nominals is the ability of Class A nominals to co-occur with a prenominal genitive. Class B nominals cannot:

(40) a. su demostración del teorema de Pitágora
    'his (agnt) proof of the theorem (objt) of Pythagorus'
  b. *su ejecución del prisionero de Juan
    'his (agnt) execution of the prisoner of Juan (objt)'

A final difference noted between class A and B nominals is that when the Genitive appears alone with class A nominals, its interpretation is ambiguous but unambiguous with class B nominals:

(41) a. su interpretación
    'his (agnt)/its (objt) interpretation'

b. su destrucción 'his (objt) destruction'

By maintaining the notion that class A nouns denote a process/event or an object (concrete or abstract) that is the result of some process and class B nouns merely denote processes/events (what Mallén calls P-nominals), Zubizarreta posits that the R-nominals of class A verbs can co-occur with a possessive while those nominals in group B cannot ever have a possessor variable. When a class A nominal denotes something concrete, the adjunct's possessive status can be interpreted either as the owner or the creator of the object (la descripción de Juan 'John's description'). If the noun denotes something abstract, the possessor is identical to the creator/agent (la interpretación de Juan 'John's interpretation'). On the contrary, the class B nouns such as *asesinato* do not have the possessive variable so when this class of nouns is found with what looks like a possessive (*su*) the only interpretation available is that of the IN-argument.

Instead of adopting Zubizarreta's nominal classifications, Mallén maintains that the difference between R-nominals and P-nominals can be attributed to a true separation between their F-head categories. According to Mallén, R-nominals are headed by the functional category QUAN while P-nominals are headed by the more Inflection-like functional element, NINFL. According to Mallén, NINFL and its event interpretation are found in complementary distribution with QUAN and its possessive variable. As has been mentioned before, according to Mallén, NINFL cannot license a possessor in [Spec, IP]. The P-nominals of class B when found with a genitive in [Spec, IP] can only have that genitive interpreted as the IN-argument of the NOUN since there is no possessor variable available in NINFL. Furthermore, Mallén adopts the characterization of Marantz (1984) that class B nominals are [-logical subject] [-transitive] which means that they never allow an EX-argument variable and cannot assign Case to their complement. Thus, the [-logical subject] feature is said to prevent assignment of an EX-argument θ-role which allows the IN-argument to raise and receive its Case from QUAN (NINFL):

(42) $[_{DP} [_{D'} \text{DET} [_{QP} \text{in-arg}_j [_{Q'} \text{QUAN} [_{N'} \text{NOUN}_{[-ls]} t_j]]]]]$

The R-nominals headed by QUAN have a possessor variable available which provides for either a possessor/owner or agent of the action interpretation of the nominal as we can see in example (43):

(43) su descripción del paisaje

Structurally in a phrase like (43), Mallén claims that for the owner interpretation *su* is generated in [Spec, QP] but for the agent interpretation, *su* raises from [Spec, NP] to [Spec, QP] for the assignment of genitive Case from QUAN:

(44) $[_{DP}$ Spec $[_{D'}$ DET $[_{QP}$ ex-arg$_j$ $[_{Q'}$ QUAN $[_{NP}$ t$_j$ $[_{N'}$ Noun in-arg]]]]]]

By using this division between the two interpretations of *su*, Mallén accounts syntactically for the differences in their usage.

4.7. DISCUSSION OF MALLEN

In this section, we will critically examine Mallén's approach to the possessive, in a general sense and as it accounts for the facts in Spanish.

Beginning with the characterization of QUAN as parameterized as to its ability to assign Case leftward or rightward, his proposal for English follows the typical characterization of functional categories. That is to say, functional categories are thought to assign Case to the left and the element receiving Case from a functional category must undergo a raising movement to acquire this Case. But if QUAN, as Mallén suggests, assigns Case to the right in Spanish, that behavior is normally associated with a lexical category and is anomalous with respect to the other functional categories like COMP and INFL.

Another difference between the functional categories such as COMP and INFL and Mallén's QUAN category is that the 'uniqueness' of the complements selected by QUAN and DET is not as unique as that of INFL which selects only for VP and COMP which selects only for IP. The fact that QUAN and DET can select for NP, CP, VP, and DP is counter evidence to the uniqueness-of-complement characterization of functional categories.

Another problem is Mallén's use of the term QUAN as a general term when he is actually referring to his more specific parallel term NINFL and vice versa. In fact, as was shown in (21), he posits two NINFLs when one, as the head of the phrase, would seem to suffice.

Two things are worthy of note with regard to the examples in (24) a and e, repeated here as (45) a and b.

(45) a. su retrato de Gertrude Stein
'his (agnt) portrait of Gertrude Stein (objt)'
b. su (poss) retrato de Gertrude Stein (objt) de Picasso (agnt)

'his (poss) portrait of Gertrude Stein by Picasso'

First, in (45a) *su* does not have to be interpreted as the agent. It could also be considered a possessor with no loss of grammaticality to the sentence. And in (45b), *su retrato de Picasso (agnt) de Gertrude Stein (objt)* is also grammatical. Although Mallén does provide empirical evidence that the distinction between agents and possessors may be needed, he does not account for these particular interpretations.

With respect to other examples given by Mallén, (36c), repeated here as (46), seems to be able to have either an agent or possessor interpretation for *Chomsky*:

(46) ??? I have never understood Chomsky's bunch of proposals.

Although the example itself may cause the ambiguity, I used my own Spanish version of (46) shown in (47) with native speaker informants. I was told that *Chomsky* could either be the possessor or the maker of the proposals, just as in English.

(47) Nunca he entendido el montón de propuestas de Chomsky.

And the nouns such as those in (32), which are considered to be 'group' nouns occupying QUAN, seem to be very limited in number. It may be a selectional restriction rather than a filled QUAN which specifies the group noun's ability to co-occur with a possessive.

There are problems with the construction that Mallén proposes for QUAN in (26), repeated below as (48), and the statement that DETs select for QUAN in unmarked cases.

(48)
```
              DP
             /  \
          Spec   D'
                /  \
              DET   QP
                   /  \
                  Q'   Spec
                 / \    |
             QUAN   NP  de-phrase(Poss)
             /  \    |
         QUAN  AGR   N'
                    / \
                 NOUN  EX-arg
                        |
                       IN-arg de-phrase
                        |
                       de-phrase
```

First, a phrase such as *todos mis amigos* ' all my friends' or *todo el mundo* 'everyone' has the quantifier element *todo* preceding the possessive or determiner. These simple phrases directly contradict Mallén's structure in (48) where the Quantifier element is lower in the tree than the determiner or possessive. Also locating the possessive in the Spec of QP is suspicious since possessives do not seem to quantify anything but rather qualify the NP. Finally, if a determiner has a QUAN in unmarked cases, that should imply that an NP without a quantifier is somehow a marked structure, a notion that seems counterintuitive.

An additional problem with Mallén's proposal is that with an agentive *by* phrase in English, the examples in (35) are fine. It appears that it is simply the translation from Spanish to English with *de* 'of' which creates the ungrammaticality. I include a similar singular example in case the possessive morpheme is obscured by the plural noun:

(49) a. He sold these students' books by Vargas Llosa.
  b. He sold this student's book by Vargas Llosa.

A further problem with Mallén's analysis lies in the classification of determiners, quantifiers, and nouns as weak Case assigners in Spanish which need the assistance of what Mallén calls the null preposition *of*. This classification of weak Case assigners is not clearly explained in his work. He also calls the French definite article more quantifier-like than that of other Romance languages but fails to provide evidence for this description.

Finally, Mallén's characterization of R- versus P-nominals is confusing and not as explanatory as the division of nominals proposed by Zubizarreta. The confusion arises from Mallén's use of his own terms combined with a discussion of Zubizarreta's classification of class A and B P-nominals. However, Mallén's examples using his characterization of the differences between R- and P-nominals are not sufficient to prove his restrictions on P-nominals as seen in (38). Using another P-nominal such as *casamiento* 'marriage' in (38a) produces total grammaticality and native speaker informants also accepted (38a) as given above. And in spite of semantic deviance, the other restrictions Mallén places on P-nominals do not always hold true with other examples. His proposal for the two types of nominals is not shown to be superior to that of Zubizarreta, since his examples do not prove that P-nominals are different than R-nominals with regard to possessives.

On a more positive note, Mallén's notion of the prenominal possessive in Spanish as a clitic is attractive because as we saw in Chapter Three, this possessive cannot govern an empty category. However, on the whole, Mallén's proposal does not provide enough evidence that two intermediate categories, QUAN and NINFL, are truly necessary to account for the empirical evidence in Spanish possessives.

4.8. CONTRERAS' DISCUSSION OF POSSESSIVES HEADING EMPTY NOMINALS

As we saw in Chapter Three, the ability of a determiner in Spanish to govern an empty category does not extend to prenominal possessives. For example, the following sentence provided by Contreras (1989) is not grammatical because the empty N' is not properly governed:

(50) *Su libro sobre Borges es mejor que su [$_{N'}$ e] sobre Cortázar.
  'His/her book on Borges is better than his/her [book] on Cortázar.'

Contreras wants to do more than just state that possessives cannot be proper governors and he begins by noting that there are two types of possessives in Spanish: those that can appear before the noun and those that follow it:

(51) a. su vaso 'his/her glass'
  b. el vaso suyo 'his/her glass'

Another item which Contreras notes with regard to the prenominal possessives in Spanish is that they have a definite interpretation unlike their postnominal counterparts which can appear with an indefinite as well as a definite article:

(52) un vaso suyo 'a glass of his/hers'

Because of this, (51) a and b are equivalent to each other but (51a) cannot be interpreted as the indefinite (52). Contreras provides the following structure to account for a possible derivation of (51a) from (51b):

(53)

```
              DP
            /    \
           D      N'
           |     /  \
         [+def] N'   A
          ↑     |
          |     N
          |     |
          |    vaso  su(yo)
          └─────────┘
```

This structure suggests that *su* [$_{N'}$ e] may be ungrammatical because as posited by Wahl (1984), lexical government of an empty category is required and an unindexed empty category cannot serve as a proper governor. Contreras states that in accordance with this proposal, the trace of *su*, after moving to the prenominal position D, has no proper governor if N' is empty. This is illustrated in (54):

(54) [$_{DP}$ su$_i$ [$_{N'}$ e] e$_i$]

By assuming the structure in (54), Contreras can then propose that any head of a determiner phrase in Spanish will be able to properly govern an empty category. Even more generally, all functional heads in Spanish can be considered proper governors. This, however, is not true in English; all heads of QP are said to be proper governors but not all heads of DP can serve in this capacity. The functional head *'s* can properly govern but no other determiner can. In order to differentiate between the lexical categories which can serve as proper governors and those that cannot (V, A, and N can; P cannot), Contreras revises Stowell's Head Government Requirement (HGR) that we saw proposed in Chapter Three:

(55) [e] must be head governed by a proper governor.

In summary, he accounts for the ungrammaticality of (50) by deriving the so-called short form of the possessive in Spanish from its long form counterpart, thus retaining its definite denotation and neatly accounting for the empirical evidence.

4.9. DISCUSSION OF CONTRERAS

Contreras' account of prenominal possessives is a simple yet very attractive proposal that correctly predicts the inability of forms like *su* to properly govern an empty category. The only change I would make is in the characterization of the Spanish determiner as a functional category. I will continue to advance my hypothesis that it is a lexical category in Spanish for all of the reasons previously given in this work. These reasons will be reviewed below. Even with the categorization of the determiner as lexical, we still retain Contreras' generalization that all functional categories (COMP and INFL) are able to properly govern in Spanish and we simply add the determiner to the list of Spanish lexical categories able to properly govern.

4.10. THE POSSESSIVE DETERMINER AS LEXICAL CATEGORY

In previous chapters, I have argued that Spanish determiners are lexical rather than functional heads, on the basis of (a) directionality of government, (b) their ability to properly govern, and (c) their ability to assign rightward Case in constructions such as *ese vaso suyo*.

In this section, I will propose my own structure for the possessive in Spanish that can account for all of its instantiations without the need for positing extra intermediate categories.

Unlike Abney and Fukui and Speas, I will continue to argue for the determiner as a lexical category. This allows for rightward Case assignment in Spanish and the proper government of empty categories. Because of this characterization of the Spanish determiner as lexical, it is not necessary to posit the same raising strategy as needed to account for the English genitive. Instead, I will propose the alternative structure seen in (56):

(56)
```
         D'
        /  \
       D    N'
       |   /  \
      los  N   Spec
           |    |
         libros míos
```

As stated in Chapter Two, the Spec of a category can be generated either on the right or the left. The rightward Spec in (56) accounts for the long form of the Spanish possessive without the need for any intermediate categories.

To account for Spanish possessives such as *el libro de Juan*, the simple structure in (57) is proposed:

(57)
```
         D'
        /  \
       D    N'
       |    |\
       el   N  PP
            |  | \
          libro P  N
                |  |
                de Juan
```

As mentioned in section 4.8, Contreras' proposal regarding the lack of proper government by prenominal possessives will be adopted with the provision that we treat the Spanish determiner as a lexical category. His derivation of the short form of the possessive from its longer counterpart will be maintained thus accounting for the last of the three ways in which the Spanish possessive can be realized.

4.11. Conclusions

In this chapter, we have seen that Abney and Fukui and Speas' proposal of genitive Case as assigned by a functional category *'s* works well in English but is not applicable to Spanish. And Mallén's hypothesis concerning the need for an intermediate node, either NINFL or QUAN, is not justified if we consider the determiner in Spanish as a lexical category. Finally, Contreras' proposal dealing with the inability of a prenominal possessive to properly govern an empty category in Spanish was seen as an elegant manner in which to account for this phenomenon. By retaining Contreras' account of prenominal possessives with the stipulation that the Spanish determiner is lexical, not functional and by proposing two other structures which easily account for the other two ways in which the Spanish possessive is realized, we can maintain the notion of the possessive as a lexical determiner just as we accounted for the definite article and demonstrative in Chapter Three.

NOTES TO CHAPTER 4

1 Exceptions are the quantifiers *many*, *several*, *few*, and *every*: John's every book.

2 Contreras (p.c.) notes that this is limited to interaction among genitive phrases: cf. Esta es una materia en que$_i$ [la competencia t$_i$ de María] es inefable. 'This is a subject in which María's competence is ineffable.'

3 Again, this is limited to genitives: Esta es la materia en la que [su competencia t] es inefable. 'This is the subject in which her competence is ineffable.'

4 Abney does not need to distinguish between the lexical category's EX-argument and the Possessor position because in English, agents and possessives are in complementary distribution:

(i) *They stole that collector's drawings of Picasso's.

5 Differing opinions are offered by Williams (1987) and Rappaport (1983) who believe that there should be no distinction made between agents and possessives because the semantic link between a possessor and its lexical head is broad enough to also include that of the agent toward the noun which assigns it a θ-role.

Chapter 5

Conclusions

In this chapter, I will provide a brief summary of the claims and proposals made in previous chapters of this work.

We began with a general discussion of the Government-Binding theory, the framework in which this study is set. The modules of that theory which pertain to the work were outlined and the definitions necessary for the reading of subsequent chapters were supplied.

In the following chapter, we dealt with concerns specific to current theory regarding determiner phrases. For the structure of determiner phrases, we adopted Abney's DP hypothesis which claims that the noun phrase is actually a phrase headed by a determiner. This determiner is said to be a functional category parallel to the functional categories COMP and INFL. The characteristics of functional versus lexical categories proposed by Abney as well as Fukui and Speas were discussed at length. Principally motivated by reasons of iteration and government, I chose to categorize the determiner in Spanish as a lexical rather than a functional category and I provided the structure to account for that categorization.

In Chapter Three, we specifically examined the determiner phrase which is headed by a definite article or demonstrative. The similarities and differences of these two types of determiners were examined in light of both Spanish and English data. The determiner phrase which lacks an overt N, a Spanish construction which English does not have, was explored in detail. Analyses by Torrego, Bosque, and Contreras of these elliptical phrases were considered. Contreras' approach to these phrases, due to ECP considerations, was shown to provide the best account of the empirical evidence. The ability of the determiner (with the exception of the possessive) to govern an empty category to its right was seen as additional evidence for my proposal that in Spanish the determiner is a lexical category.

Another Contreras proposal, regarding the proper government of noun phrases which appear in subject position without an overt determiner, was also discussed but left unanswered questions about bare nouns in certain structures.

In Chapter Four, the determiner phrase which contains either a possessive or a genitive was discussed. The proposals by Chomsky, Abney, and Fukui and Speas for the English genitive were shown to be applicable to English but not to Spanish. The movement of a noun to the Spec of DP in order to receive the genitive Case assigned leftward by the functional element *'s* was unnecessary for Spanish, whose genitive Case assignment was better accounted for by my hypothesis that the determiner is a lexical category in Spanish. This proposal allows rightward Case assignment for the genitive with no need for the raising strategy posited for English.

Mallén's notion that the Spanish determiner phrase has intermediate nodes, QUAN and NINFL, which head their own functional phrases, was examined but rejected because it lacked explanatory value with regard to actual Spanish data.

Finally, the inability of the short form of the Spanish possessive to properly govern an empty category was explained. We saw that by the adoption of Contreras' proposal that derives *su* from the long form of the possessive, the empty N is unable to properly govern the trace of *su* which follows it. The only change I proposed for his analysis was that of the determiner as a lexical rather than a functional category in Spanish.

In this study, I have shown that the ability of determiners to iterate, to govern empty categories, and to assign rightward Case are better accounted for by viewing the Spanish determiner as a lexical category rather than a functional one.

Bibliography

Abney, Steven. 1986. Functional Elements and Licensing, paper presented to GLOW 1986, Girona, Spain.
_____. 1987. The English Noun Phrase in its Sentential Aspect. Doctoral dissertation, MIT.
Aoun, Joseph, and Dominique Sportiche. 1983. On the Formal Theory of Government. Linguistic Review 2.211-36.
Aristotle. The Poetics, published 1939, with a translation by W. Hamilton Fyfe, Loeb Classical Library, Cambridge, MA: Harvard University Press.
Baker, Mark C. 1988. Incorporation: A Theory of Grammatical Function Changing. Chicago: University of Chicago Press.
Bello, Andrés. 1847. Gramática de la lengua castellana. With notes by R. Cuervo, prologue and notes by N. Alcalá-Zamora y Torres, 8th ed. Buenos Aires: Editorial Sopena Argentina, 1970.
Borer, Hagit. 1986. I-subjects. Linguistic Inquiry 17.375-416.
Bosque, Ignacio. 1986. Constricciones morfológicas sobre la coordinación. ms., Universidad Complutense, Madrid.
Brame, Michael. 1981. The General Theory of Binding and Fusion. Linguistic Analysis 7.277-325.
Chomsky, Noam. 1970. Remarks on Nominalization. Readings in English Transformational Grammar, ed. by R. Jacobs and P. Rosenbaum. The Hague: Mouton.
_____. 1981. Lectures on Government and Binding. Dordrecht: Foris.
_____. 1982. Some Concepts and Consequences of the Theory of Government and Binding. Cambridge, MA: MIT Press.
_____. 1986a. Knowledge of Language: Its Nature, Origins, and Use. New York: Praeger.
_____. 1986b. Barriers. Cambridge, MA: MIT Press.
Contreras, Heles. 1986. Spanish Bare NPs and the ECP. Generative Studies in Spanish Syntax, ed. by Ivonne Bordelois, Heles Contreras, and Karen Zagona, 25-49. Dordrecht: Foris.
_____. 1989. On Spanish Empty N' and N*. Current Issues in Linguistic Theory, ed. by Carl Kirschner and Janet DeCesaris, 83-95. Amsterdam: Benjamins.
Emonds, Joseph. 1985. A Unified Theory of Syntactic Categories. Dordrecht: Foris.

Fukui, Naoki. 1986. A Theory of Category Projection and Its Applications. Doctoral dissertation, MIT.
_____ and Margaret Speas. 1986. Specifiers and Projection. MIT Working Papers in Linguistics 8.128-72.
Haik, Isabelle. 1982. On Clitic *en* in French. Journal of Linguistic Research, 63-87.
Huang, C.-T. James. 1982. Logical Relations in Chinese and the Theory of Grammar. Doctoral dissertation, MIT.
Kayne, Richard. 1981a. ECP Extensions. Linguistic Inquiry 12.93-133.
_____. 1981b. On Certain Differences Between French and English. Linguistic Inquiry 12.349-71.
Koopman, Hilda and Dominique Sportiche. 1982. Variables and the Bijection Principle. The Linguistic Review 2.139-60.
Lees, R.B. 1960. The Grammar of English Nominalizations. The Hague: Mouton.
Lobeck, Anne. 1986. Syntactic Constraints on VP Ellipsis. Doctoral dissertation, University of Washington.
Makino, S. 1968. Some Aspects of Japanese Nominalizations. Tokyo: Tokai University Press.
Mallén, Enrique. 1988. Extraction from Spanish Noun Phrases. To appear in Natural Language and Linguistic Theory.
Marantz, Alec. 1984. On the Nature of Grammatical Relations. Linguistic Inquiry Monograph No. 10. Cambridge, MA: MIT Press.
Montalbetti, M. 1984. After Binding: On the Interpretation of Pronouns. Doctoral dissertation, MIT.
Napoli, Donna J. 1985. Verb Phrase Deletion in English: A Base-generated Analysis. Journal of Linguistics 21.281-319.
Rappaport, Malka. 1983. On the Nature of Derived Nominals. Papers in Lexical-Functional Grammar, ed. by L. Levin, M. Rappaport, and A. Zaenen. Indiana University Linguistics Club.
Reinhart, Tanya. 1983. Anaphora and Semantic Interpretation. Chicago: University of Chicago Press.
Rivero, María Luisa. 1986. Binding in NPs. Generative Studies in Spanish Syntax, ed. by Ivonne Bordelois, Heles Contreras, and Karen Zagona, 165-82.
Roeper, Thomas. 1984. Implicit Arguments and the Projection Principle. ms., University of MA, Amherst.
Solé, Carlos and Yolanda Solé. 1977. Modern Spanish Syntax: A Study in Contrast. Lexington, MA: D.C. Heath and Company.

Stowell Timothy. 1981. Origins of Phrase Structure. Doctoral dissertation, MIT.

———. 1985. Null Antecedents and Proper Government. Northeastern Linguistics Society 16.476-93.

Suñer, Margarita. 1982a. The Syntax and Semantics of Presentational Type Sentences in Spanish. Washington, D.C.: Georgetown University Press.

Torrego, Esther. 1987. On Empty Categories in Nominals. ms., MIT.

Wahl, Andy. 1984. Two Types of Locality. ms., University of Maryland.

Williams, Edwin. 1987. Implicit Arguments, the Binding Theory, and Control. Natural Language and Linguistic Theory 5.151-80.

Zubizarreta, María Luisa. 1987. Levels of Representation in the Lexicon and in the Syntax. Dordrecht: Foris.

Index of Names

Abney, S., 14, 15, 16, 17, 18, 19, 20, 21, 22, 23, 24, 25, 26, 29, 31, 33, 34, 36, 37, 38, 69, 70, 71, 72, 73, 74, 80, 94, 95, 96n4, 97, 98
Aoun, J., 9
Aristotle, 23, 24

Baker, M., 4, 5, 7, 10,
Bello, A., 61
Borer, H., 47, 66n5
Bosque, I., 51, 52, 53, 54, 58, 59, 68n14, 97
Brame, M., 13

Chomsky, N., 1, 2, 3, 4, 5, 7, 8, 9, 12n1, 17, 21, 26, 30, 46, 48, 51, 52, 53, 55, 66n6, 67n9, 69, 70, 76, 79, 98
Contreras, H., 38n1, 41, 51, 53, 54, 55, 56, 57, 58, 59, 60, 61, 62, 63, 64, 65, 66, 67n10, 67n11, 68n14, 68n15, 69, 92, 93, 94, 95, 96n2, 97, 98

Emonds, J., 33

Fukui, N., 14, 26, 27, 28, 29, 30, 31, 34, 35, 36, 37, 38, 56, 57, 59, 69, 74, 75, 77, 78, 94, 95, 97, 98

Haik, I., 67n8
Huang, J., 67n13

Kayne, R., 60, 64, 67n13
Koopman, H., 59, 67n12

Lees, R., 16, 17
Lobeck, A., 53, 54, 58, 59

Makino, 39n3
Mallén, E., 12, 69, 77, 79, 80, 81, 82, 83, 84, 85, 86, 87, 88, 89, 90, 91, 92, 95, 98
Marantz, A., 88
Montalbetti, M., 50

Napoli, D., 67n11

Rappaport, M., 96n5
Rivero, M., 81
Roeper, T., 25

Solé, C., 41
Solé, Y., 41
Speas, M., 14, 26, 27, 28, 29, 30, 31, 34, 35, 36, 37, 38, 56, 57, 59, 69, 74, 75, 77, 78, 94, 95, 97, 98
Sportiche, D., 9, 59, 67n12
Stowell, T., 21, 55, 93
Suñer, M., 62
Suzuki, 23, 24

Torrego, E., 41, 44, 45, 46, 47, 48, 49, 50, 55, 66, 66n2, 66n3, 66n5, 66n6, 67n7, 67n8, 97

Wahl, A., 93
Williams, E., 96n5

Zubizarreta, M., 86, 87, 88. 92

Index of Subjects

Adjunction, 29
Agent, 80, 84, 86, 88, 89, 90, 96n4, 96n5
Agreement (AGR),15, 33, 34, 36, 46, 47, 48, 51, 66n4, 71, 73, 83
  See also under Case, Spec-head agreement
Anaphors, 10, 11
  See also under Binding Theory, Government and Binding Theory
Antecedent, 10, 11, 49, 66n8
Argument, 7, 78, 81
  external (EX), 78, 79, 80, 88, 96n4
  internal (IN), 78, 79, 80, 88
  See also under Theta

Barrier, 9, 29, 30, 31, 48, 78
Binding Theory, 10-11, 49, 55
  See also under Government and Binding Theory, Principles and Parameters

C-Command, 6, 9, 12n1, 30, 49, 67n8, 80
Case Theory, 8-9
  See also under Case, Principles and Parameters
Case, 8, 17, 19, 51, 76, 77, 80, 81, 88, 98
  accusative, 8
  assignment, 19, 56, 69, 72, 76, 77, 80, 89, 91, 94, genitive, 29, 31, 33, 35, 38, 56, 69, 70, 71, 72, 73, 74, 75, 78, 80, 89, 95, 98
  inherent, 9
  lexical, 29
  marking, 35, 36, 70, 72
  nominative, 8, 29, 56, 80
  oblique, 8
  structural, 9, 77
Catalan, 44
Chains, 3, 8, 70
Clitic, 45, 50, 67n10, 81, 92
Clitic doubling construction, 38
Closed Class, 13, 28, 33, 35
Coindexation, 13
Complement, 4, 7, 20, 21, 34, 35, 36, 83, 88
Complementary distribution, 72, 73, 74, 96n4
Complementizer (COMP), 5, 26, 28, 30, 33, 35, 45, 78, 89, 94, 97
Complementizer phrase (CP), 47
Control Restrictions, 18
Control Theory, 11
Coreference, 11

D-structure, 2, 3, 29, 30, 70, 72, 81, 83
Definite article, 14, 35, 38, 41, 45, 46, 48, 69, 72, 73, 93, 96, 97
  gender and number of, 42, 66
  in English, 14, 51, 53, 60, 66
  in Spanish, 14, 45, 47, 50,

51, 52, 53, 60, 66, 67n10,
67n11
  in subject position, 60
  omission of, 42, 43
  uses of, 43
  without a noun, 43, 50
Definiteness, 71
Demonstrative, 14, 33, 35, 38,
  41, 45, 47, 50, 69, 96, 97
  in Spanish, 46, 51, 52
Determiner Phrase (DP)
  Hypothesis, 14, 15, 18,
  20, 31, 70, 97
Determiner Phrases (DPs), 13,
  14, 15, 16, 18, 19, 21, 31,
  33, 34, 35, 38, 44, 47, 48,
  58, 66, 67n7, 77, 79, 86,
  97, 98
  empty, 59
  extraction from, 30
  in English, 14, 16, 34, 93
  in Spanish, 14, 31, 33, 34,
  92, 98
  structure, 20, 21, 28, 37,
  56, 93, 97
Determiners, 13, 14, 15, 16,
  20, 31, 34, 35, 36, 37, 38,
  38n2, 41, 46, 51, 56, 57,
  59, 64, 72, 73, 75, 77, 78,
  80, 83, 89, 90, 91, 94, 96,
  97, 98
  as functional head, 57, 74,
  78
  as lexical category, 68n15,
  72, 73, 94, 95, 96, 97, 98
  elision, 71, 73
  empty, 61, 71
  numerical, 73
  See also under English,
Functional Category,
Lexical Category, Spanish
Directionality, 81, 94
Distinctive Features, 2

El nominal construction, 44,
  45, 46, 47, 49, 50, 51,
  67n8
Empty category (EC), 52, 54,
  55, 56, 57, 59, 60, 65, 66,
  67n10, 67n11, 67n12, 69,
  92, 93, 94, 95, 98
Empty Category Principle
  (ECP), 9-10, 46, 51, 55,
  57, 59, 60, 61, 62, 63, 65,
  66, 97
English, 4, 5-6, 8, 9, 14, 16,
  35, 41, 42, 65, 71, 73, 74,
  78, 80, 84, 90, 91, 93, 95,
  96n4, 97
  See also under
  Determiners, Functional
  Category, Lexical
  Category, Spanish
Ergative verbs, 60
Este nominal, 45, 46, 47, 50,
  51

F-features, 29, 31, 56, 75
F-selection, 22, 28, 86
French, 46, 47, 51, 52, 66n4,
  67n10, 79, 91
Functional (F) Categories, 14,
  19, 20, 21, 22, 23, 24, 25,
  26, 27, 28, 29, 30, 31, 33,
  34, 35, 36, 38, 39n5, 41,
  51, 56, 68n15, 77, 78, 88,
  89, 94, 95, 97, 98
Functional head, 30, 56, 57,

Functional head, 30, 56, 57, 59, 78, 81, 83, 86, 88, 93, 94
Functional Projection Theorem, 56

Genitives, 19, 72, 75, 87, 88, 96n2, 96n3, 98
   as case assigners, 19, 29, 69
   in English, 67n11, 69, 70, 74, 75, 76, 94, 98
   in Spanish, 69, 72, 74, 76, 78, 98
   marking, 29
   structure, 95
Govern, 28, 35, 38, 49, 67n9, 78, 80, 98
Governing Category, 10, 11
Government and Binding Theory, 1, 2, 3, 4, 11, 97
   modules, 1, 4, 11, 97
Government, K(ayne), 64
Government, lexical, 93
Government, proper, 51, 52, 53, 54, 57, 58, 59, 60, 64, 67n13, 68n14, 68n15, 69, 92, 93, 94, 95, 98
Government, theory of, 9, 64, 66n6, 97

Head First Language, 4, 78
Head government, 57
Head Government Requirement (HGR), 55, 59, 93-94
Head Last Language, 4
Heads, 5, 79, 89
Hebrew, 66n5
Hungarian, 72

Indefinite article, 93
Inflection (INFL), 5, 8, 11, 20, 21, 22, 26, 33, 34, 35, 53, 60, 63, 74, 78, 80, 89. 94, 97
Inflectional Phrase (IP), 5, 9, 22, 28, 29, 53
   tensed, 8
Intermediate Phrases, 12, 77, 78, 94, 95, 98
Italian, 35, 38, 44, 46, 47, 51, 79, 84
Iteration, 27, 36, 38, 39n4, 78, 97, 98
   See also under Functional Category, Lexical Category

Japanese, 4, 34, 35, 39n5

Kase, 19, 27, 28, 29, 30, 31, 56, 75, 77

Language acquisition, 79
Leonese dialect, 35, 38
Levels of Representation, 2, 3, 4
Lexical Categories, 4, 14, 15, 20, 22, 26, 27, 28, 33, 35, 36, 38, 41, 50, 51, 56, 57, 59, 60, 64, 69, 75, 89, 93, 94, 95, 96n4, 97, 98
Lexical Head, 15, 30, 59, 83, 84, 96n5
Lexical (L) marking, 30
Lexicalist Hypothesis, 79
Lexically Based Syntax, 13
Lexicon, 2, 3
Logical Form (LF), 2, 3, 39n4

M-command, 9, 12n1
Maximal Projection, 5, 53, 56, 59, 60, 78
Modification, 86
Move Alpha, 2, 3
   LF, 2
   syntactic, 3, 7, 10
Movement, 29, 33, 61, 70, 77, 78, 98

N bar (N'), 17, 18, 58
   empty, 64, 92, 93
NINFL (nominal INFL), 77, 78, 83, 88, 89, 92, 95, 98
   structure, 78
Nominals, 88
   class A, 87, 88, 92
   class B, 87, 88, 92
   empty, 10, 41, 45, 48, 49, 50, 51, 52, 53, 57, 59. 66, 66n2
   headed by a definite article, 45
   headed by a demonstrative, 45
   in phrases, 17, 55, 67n11, 81, 84
Nonlexical Categories, 5
Noun, 41, 70, 77, 79, 80, 88, 91, 92, 96n5
   bare in subject position, 65
   empty, 53, 55, 58, 98
   focused bare, 62
   group, 83, 86, 87, 90
   mass, 62, 65
   plural bare, 62
   plural generic, 43
   proper, 43
   syntactic functions, 41, 60

   without a determiner, 41, 66
Noun Phrase (NP), 13, 14, 15, 16, 17, 18, 19, 20, 31, 34, 38n2, 44, 45, 47, 50, 51, 61, 64, 70, 76, 77, 79, 80, 81, 91, 97, 98
   adverbs, 77
   bare subject NPs, 60, 61, 62, 63, 64, 66
   complement, 28, 86
   empty, 36, 44. 47, 48, 51, 59
   focused, 62, 63, 65
   in English, 32, 71
   in Spanish, 32, 41, 64, 65
   nonfocused, 62
   plural, 61, 65
   singular, 61
   structure, 60, 78
   without determiners, 61, 98
Numeral, 52-53

Operator, 55

Parametric Variation, 4, 9
Parallelism Condition, 63, 64
Phonological Form (PF), 2, 3, 73
P-nominals, 86-87, 88, 92
Portuguese, 44
Possessives, 16, 21, 34, 35, 38, 52, 59, 66, 67n10, 69, 70, 71, 72, 73, 78, 79, 80, 81, 83, 84, 86, 87, 88, 89, 90, 91, 92, 94, 96, 96n4, 96n5
   agentive, 84
   alienable, 84
   inalienable, 84

in Spanish, 69, 74, 78, 92, 94, 95, 96
  long form, 72, 94, 95, 98
  prenominal, 92, 93, 94, 95
  phrases, 38, 75, 77, 98
  pronominal, 81
  postnominal, 93
  short form, 94, 95, 98
Predication, 18, 25
Preposition, 44, 47, 67n13, 75, 87
  insertion of, 19, 76, 77, 80
  null, 91
  use of *de* in Spanish, 44, 47, 51, 75, 80
Principles and Parameters, 1
PRO, 11-12, 46, 48
  controlled, 12, 32
  infinitive, subject of, 11
  in NP, 20, 24, 34
  uncontrolled, 14, 25
pro, 11, 44, 46, 47, 48, 49, 50, 51, 66n5, 67n8
Projection Principle, 3
Projections, 5
Pronouns, 10, 50, 67n11
  bound, 66n8
Pseudo-topic constructions, 61

QUAN, 77, 78, 80, 81, 83, 86, 87, 88, 89, 90, 92, 95, 98
  in English, 78
  in Spanish, 78
Quantifier (Q), 34, 37, 58, 59, 78, 80, 83, 87, 91, 96n1
  as head of phrase, 57, 58, 93
  empty, 60, 62, 63, 64, 65

phrase (QP) structure, 58, 78, 84

Referential (R) expressions, 10-11
R-nominals, 86, 88, 92
Relative clause, 45, 47, 73

S-structure, 2, 3, 24, 29, 47, 67n8, 72, 81, 86
Selectional restrictions, 77, 90
Sentence, 16, 17, 18, 19, 78
Spanish, 4, 5, 9, 10, 11, 13, 14, 41, 42, 43, 44, 75, 77, 78, 79, 80, 81, 84, 90, 94, 95, 97, 98
  as a VOS language, 60, 65
  SVO word order, 61
  See also under
    Determiners, English, Functional Category, Lexical Category
Spec-head agreement, 51-52, 53, 67n9, 80
  See also under Agreement, Government
Specifier (Spec), 21, 26, 27, 28, 30, 31, 34, 35, 37, 38, 39n4, 51, 52, 53, 54, 58, 59, 67n11, 68n14, 70, 74, 77, 79, 86, 91, 95, 98
Subcategorization, 2, 3
Subject, 14, 16, 17, 18, 53, 63
Syntactic Levels, 3
Syntactic Structure, 4

Theta (θ), 25, 79
  assignment, 71, 81

Thematic Categories, 14, 23,
    24, 33
Theta grid, 79
Thematic Relations, 2, 6
Theta (θ) Criterion, 7
Theta Index, 8
Theta Marking, 30, 70
Theta (θ) Roles, 6-7, 77, 80,
    84, 96n5
    external, 6-7, 88
    internal, 6-7
Theta (θ) Theory, 6-7, 77
Topic construction, 63, 64
    position, 62, 63, 65, 67n8
Traces, 3, 7, 10, 11, 81, 83

Uniqueness of complement, 89
Universal Grammar, 1, 2, 10,
    11, 29
Universal Principles, 2

Variable, 56, 67n12, 87
    bound, 67n8
    coindexed, 63, 64
    EX-argument, 88
    NP, 63
    possessive, 86, 88
Verb, 15, 23, 79
Visibility Condition on LF, 8,
    78

+WH COMP, 56
+WH Elements, 3, 5, 10, 29,
    30, 56

X' Theory, 4, 5, 6, 9, 17, 20,
    21, 31